CALIFORNIA WINERIES

San Luis Obispo ❖ Santa Barbara ❖ Ventura

Photographer
HARA PHOTOGRAPHICS

Author
VICKI LEÓN

Designer
ASHALA NICOLS-LAWLER

©1986 Blake Publishing Inc.
2222 Beebee Street, San Luis Obispo, California 93401.
All rights reserved.
Printed in the United States of America.
ISBN 0-918303-06-0
Volume 1 in a series

*This is California's coastal heart.
A soft land whose shoulders are vine-velveted,
oak-dotted, fog-nourished...*

A coastal land whose ocean breezes glide along the curve of river valleys to cool and caress the vines...

A flower-bright land of missions, mountain peaks and misty vistas, whose wines are as graceful as the terrain.

Introduction

California's best-kept secret may well be the wineries that flourish throughout San Luis Obispo, Santa Barbara and Ventura Counties. Winery exploration in this tawny terrain of snug hills and valleys has the quality of a small expedition. The land feels fresh, untrodden. You set forth on lupine-lined country roads, each with the hint of a small *eureka!* around the next bend. Wineries here don't trumpet their presence with huge signs. Instead, they beckon from hilltops or peek through distant trees.

Until the mid-1970s, winemaking in these counties was a modest affair. Then the vines began to go in. Each year, area wines and grapes win more acclaim. And winemakers add: "Our art — and our vines — are young. The best is yet to come."

Why has this region become so grape happy? In a word: climate. Grape experts have identified dozens of local microclimates, or pockets of favored terrain. Classified according to temperature, these Region I

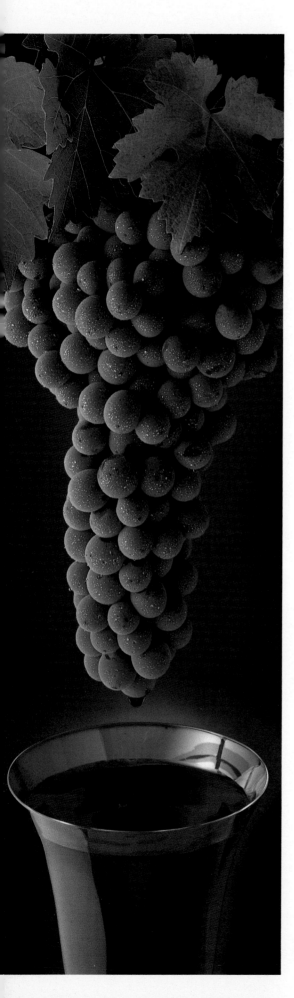

II and III microclimates are ideal for growing Chardonnay, Cabernet Sauvignon and other noble grapes.

The welcoming spirit of the land also plays a part. This is a region that delights in its rural qualities. People have different priorities here. Most of them believe that the vista of a vineyard running to meet the horizon is infinitely more beautiful than a subdivision.

There is an unmistakable family feeling about wineries in California's coastal heart. Like the great chateaux of France, most of them produce under 20,000 cases a year. Once inside their tasting rooms, you are easily drawn into the circle of unhurried tasters and talkers. That pleasant person pouring you another drop could just as likely be the owner as the winemaker — often one and the same. The mystique of hands-on winemaking attracts an unusual breed: bright, sophisticated people, unafraid of hard work. Most see themselves as caretakers of the grape, there to choose the best berries and gently nudge them toward their transformation into the jewel of beverages.

This book about the winemakers and wineries of California's coastal heart has three aims. The first is practical: to serve as a photographic guide for touring, tasting and armchair sampling. Six road maps and an index-directory help make route planning and reference a snap.

The book's second aim is historical: to survey and celebrate more than 50 of the most talented winemakers in the area. It takes dreamers who are also doers to patiently guide a living liquid to its highest potential. Why do they do it? Perhaps because winemaking is such a satisfying adventure. And why do they choose to pursue their art along this 180-mile stretch of coast? Because the vineyards of this Central Coast appellation, still in their adolescence, are already producing wines with heart. Shapely wines, wines with breadth, a palette of wines as varied and striking as the countryside.

Finally, *California Wineries* endeavors to give a sense of place, to present the landscape behind these fine wines. Besides buildings, human beings and vineyards, you'll encounter Spanish missions, tiny lakes — even a greedy raccoon or two. In these pages we've chosen to show the wineries in the context of their surroundings — surely some of the most beguiling terrain to be found anywhere. ❖

Contents

10 Paso Robles area
Near the Monterey County line sits peaceful Mission San Miguel. From the village of San Miguel south to Templeton, more than 20 wineries now thrive.

48 San Luis Obispo area
In the 1700s, Spanish missionaries planted the first wine grapes. Today their place is taken by the prime berries being grown in beautiful Edna Valley, just south of San Luis Obispo city.

64 Santa Maria area
Mission La Purísima near Lompoc symbolizes the Santa Maria area wineries. They are scattered from Nipomo to the west end of Highway 246, where the grape-growing appellations of the Santa Maria and Santa Ynez Valleys meet.

76 Santa Ynez area
Most of the wineries in the area fall within the triangle east of Highway 101. The hamlets of Buellton, Solvang, Los Olivos and Santa Ynez serve as navigation points.

108 Santa Barbara area
Santa Barbara, home of two wineries, several négociants and uncounted wine lovers, also has a noble mission overlooking the city.

116 Ventura area
Four wineries, whose styles vary from country rustic to urban sophisticated, make wine in this county. Mission San Buenaventura, in downtown Ventura, is about mid-way point.

126 Index-Directory
An alphabetical roundup of wineries and other outlets, with street addresses, tasting room hours and additional resource information.

Paso Robles
AREA

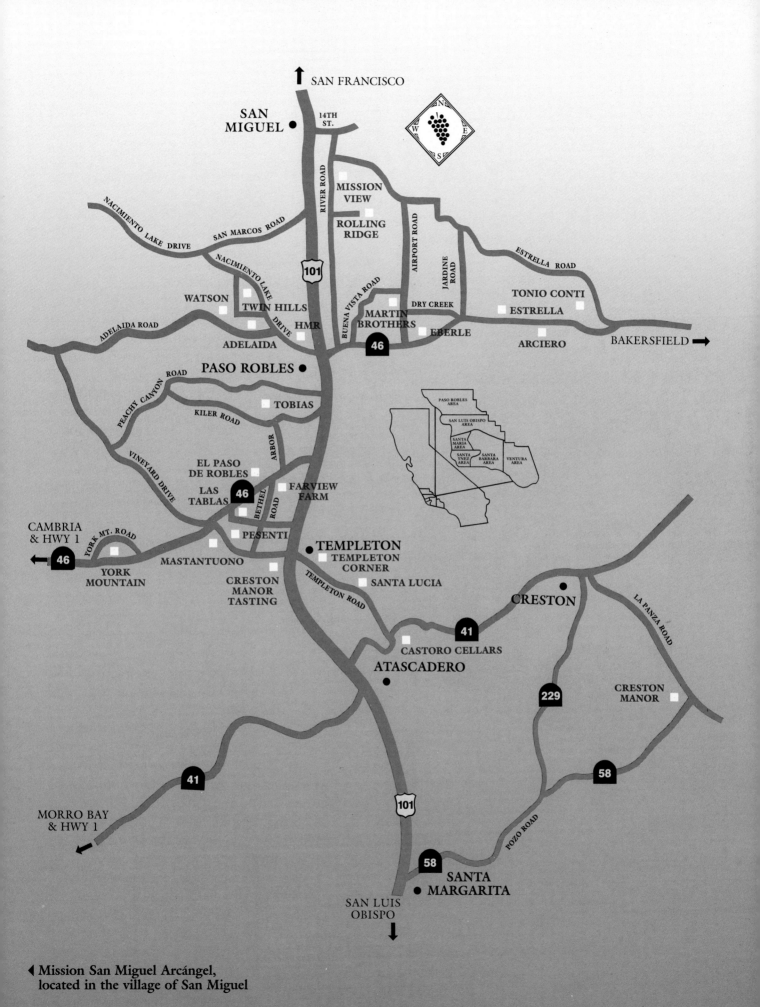

◀ Mission San Miguel Arcángel, located in the village of San Miguel

Adelaida

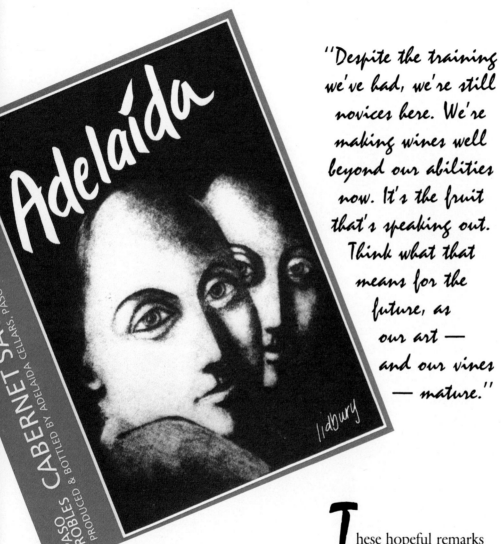

"Despite the training we've had, we're still novices here. We're making wines well beyond our abilities now. It's the fruit that's speaking out. Think what that means for the future, as our art — and our vines — mature."

These hopeful remarks come from winemaker John Munch, whose Cabernets and Chardonnays with the compelling Adelaida label have garnered golds in judgings from San Francisco to New York.

Located on a sleepy county road west of Paso Robles, Adelaida Cellars is a bonded facility which will eventually handle all aspects of winemaking. At present, John leases facilities from Estrella River Winery. He also buys grapes from Estrella and Shandon Valley and will do so even when his own few acres of French Syrah, grown for blending, begin to bear.

Now producing 6,000 cases per year, John and his French wife Andrée plan to reach 10,000 cases in 1987. From a winemaking background herself, Andrée handles marketing for the winery.

If Adelaida wines seem to project an international image, they are only echoing the Munchs' lives. John was born in Costa Rica, raised amid "way too many bananas" (his father worked for United Fruit), and studied winemaking in Europe. In between, he has mastered such diverse fields as Anglo-Saxon poetry, millworking and investment counseling.

He and Andrée met while working for a Swiss investment firm, later moving to Provence, France. It was there that English friend and artist Michael Lidbury gave them the picture which was to become their wine label. The artwork is an old etching technique called *manier noir*. Interestingly, it was Lidbury who also pointed them toward the Paso Robles region when they began hunting for the ideal place for a winery. "And we've found it," say the Munchs. ❖

Paso Robles Area

Arciero means archer in Italian, and Paso Robles is the target — in this case, for a winery which promises to be one of the largest in three coastal counties.

As you drive east on Highway 46, you see the young vines of Arciero, greening more than 500 acres. In their midst stands a 78,000-square-foot winery: dressed with stone, adorned with arches and topped with a tower in the classic Italian mode. Within its warm Mediterranean walls, Arciero Winery welcomes visitors to a range of family-oriented facilities. Built with its ageing facilities underground, visitors are able to look down onto a sea of barrels and stainless steel tanks capable of holding one million gallons of wine.

Open in mid-1986, the tasting room is part of a complex that includes a gallery devoted to rotating exhibits. One week it might be artists' handiwork. The

next, a display of game trophies. (Co-owner Phil Arciero is a big game hunter.) The following month, the gallery might hold a collection of fine racing cars — the particular *afición* of co-owner Frank Arciero and sons.

The Arciero brothers, third generation winemakers from a northern Italian family, chose this area because it was the best match to their native village of Montecasino. Still active as developers in Orange County, they hired Greg Bruni as winemaker in 1984.

"I was raised in a tasting room," says Greg, whose father and grandfather worked at San Martin Winery. A U.C. Davis graduate, Bruni became San Martin's winemaker in 1979, where he developed their first soft-style wines.

For the Arcieros, he is making Chardonnay, Sauvignon Blanc, Chenin Blanc, Zinfandel, Muscat Canelli and a white Zinfandel. He shares their philosophy and their vision. "In ten years, we'll be making 200,000 cases — and all of it the wholesome way — no additives, no herbicides. We believe this area's going to become Southern California's Wine Country." ❖

Castoro Cellars

Castoro's attention-getting label — a mischievous beaver eating grapes — has special symbolism for winemaker Niels Udsen. "I was always called 'beaver' at home — a nickname my brothers invented because they couldn't pronounce Niels. In 1975, I went to live in Italy and ended up working in a spaghetti sauce factory. Naturally, I got involved in Italian family life — and that means good red wine. I used to joke with my Italian friends and tell them: Someday, 'il castoro' ('beaver' in Italian) will have a winery too."

A scant ten years later, Castoro Cellars has become a reality. Niels' Danish wife Berit is Castoro's only full-time employee. The Udsens do not have a tasting room outlet but plan to. "When? It's a big maybe," says Berit, who goes by the euphonious nickname of Bimmer. Their wines are now sold mail order and through outlets in three counties. Castoro wine is also available at nearby Templeton Corner.

The Udsens met while at school in San Luis Obispo. During that time, they both took a shine to the grapes and wines of the Paso Robles appellation. Their 3,000 cases a year include a much-praised Cabernet Sauvignon, plus Fumé Blanc, Chardonnay, Zinfandel and a white Zin. Their goal? "To produce premium wines at prices that most people can afford — not just an elite few." ❖

Creston Manor

It may be new but Creston Manor already has stature — figuratively and literally. To get there, you follow the curves of Highway 58 as they wind east into the La Panza Mountains. At 1,700 feet, you arrive at the winery, tucked among opulent golden hills and lake-fed vineyards, the highest in San Luis Obispo County.

What are the advantages of such an elevation? Winemaker Victor Hugo Roberts responds: "Our east-west alignment and altitude actually make us into a separate, cooler growing region. As a result, our wines have more intensity and higher acid." With Creston Manor since its establishment in 1982, Roberts is a U.C. Davis graduate who was formerly with Italian-Swiss Colony and Brookside Winery.

A boutique winery whose output is deliberately kept to small lots of four choice wines, Creston Manor has already earned praise from the *cognoscenti*. Wine authority Robert Lawrence Balzar has lauded their Sauvignon Blanc and their Pinot Noir Nouveau — which he christened "November New." By the 1990s, the winery intends to be producing 50,000 cases a year, much of it estate bottled.

Four diverse personalities put together the winery and continue to lend their talents. Best-selling author Christina Crawford and her media executive husband David Koontz most enjoy bottling wine and working the vineyard. Insurance company president Larry Rosenbloom and his wife Stephanie concentrate on the public relations aspects. For all four wine lovers, the 500-acre ranch is home.

Creston Manor also has a tasting room off Highway 101 at Vineyard Drive; the winery itself makes an appetizing destination for a wine-tasting picnic and a swim in the lake. Eventually the owners plan a guesthouse-lodge on the grounds. ❖

Creston country: a soft palette of golden hills, silver water, grey-green oaks and emerald vines surrounds the winery.

EBERLE WINERY

The tasting room is a marvel — thick carpet, handsome oak wainscoting, Impressionist paintings and a fireplace of glowing garnet tile the color of Gary Eberle's favorite 1980 Cabernet. There is no sign over the entrance. If there were, it might read: "Eat, drink and be merry." That would echo the priorities of this family enterprise.

The Eberles have inaugurated gourmet dinners at the winery, held six times a year. The 6-course feasts feature local wines, foods and chefs. Dinners have included such show-stoppers as medallion of buffalo calf tenderloin.

The dinners take place in the candle-lit tasting room, whose artful design lets you admire the sunset through French doors. During regular tasting hours, visitors can admire other views as well. One interior window cuts away to a splendid panorama of the barrel and fermentation room; another lets you see the crush at close hand.

But this is not just a showplace tour-and-taste winery. It is an oenophile's winery with a short and serious list of premium drinking wines. Open since 1981, Eberle makes Cabernet Sauvignon and Chardonnay. Period. "At the pleading of my wife and daughter, I also make a small amount of Muscat Canelli and a white Cab from time to time, but that's it," says Gary. Eberle wines have garnered both critical and public acclaim. The most prestigious honor may be the 1980 Cabernet's inclusion in the 75th Anniversary Memento Wine Collection at U.C. Davis.

A native Pennsylvanian, Gary completed the enology doctoral program at U.C. Davis in 1972. After graduating, he and half-brother Cliff Giacobine established Estrella River Winery. Gary selected the Estrella varietals, made their wines and did microclimate research before

Paso Robles Area

"Funny — most of the winemakers who talk about wines as if they were their children are bachelors. I'm a father myself. And I know that the difference between wine and children is that you can sit down and reason with a bottle of Cabernet."

— Gary Eberle, winemaker

moving a couple of miles down the road to do hands-on winemaking.

Originally a teacher, wife Jeanie got involved by osmosis in tastings and wine sales at Estrella; she now runs her own business, distributing 23 area wines.

Winemaking Eberle-style might be serious business, but Eberle himself is not. A cracker of jokes as well as a maker of wine, Gary has a quip for every occasion. Daughter Darien shares her father's ways with people. When not at college, she fills in where needed in tasting, sales and promotion. "Father and daughter are both comedians, so they work well together," says Jeanie. ❖

Sign of the boar: their label depicts a small wild boar — the original meaning of "eberle" — chosen by winemaker Gary (top) and wife Jeanie (inset).

Paso Robles Area

El Paso de Robles
Winery and Vineyards

"Like a coach, I recruit grapes... I'm constantly aware of what my vines — and other vineyards in the area — can produce." George Mulder, winemaster, grape grower and grape buyer at El Paso de Robles, talks about the roles he and other family members play in this hands-on operation. "People ask me: why and how did a psychologist get into the winery business? My response is: I approach both psychology and winemaking as an artist."

His wife Tahoma ("Tomie"), who is involved in every facet of the business, sees the winery from a visitor's point of view. "People are looking for an experience, not just a destination. Here, they are able to sample agriculture's most romantic product in a nice setting and maybe learn something in the process."

Looking like a small and hospitable mission, El Paso de Robles sits amid its vines along Highway 46 west, beckoning travelers to pause awhile. (In order to do so without backtracking, you should take a left turn at Bethel Road before passing the winery.) An arbor of Zinfandel vines leads to the cool recesses of the winery. The open-beamed tasting room feels like the Mulder's living room. Big rockers frame the fireplace. A long mahogany tasting bar and bright items for sale encourage dawdling. Outside, daffodil-yellow tables and chairs let wine-tasters gaze over an 11-acre expanse of vines.

Bonded since 1981, the winery makes an ambitious list of seven reds, a blush and two white wines. The Merlot and Zinfandels have already taken awards.

Both educators, the Mulders were part of a group of local families who took up home winemaking in the 1970s. To learn commercial winemaking, the Mulders attended classes in enology at U.C. Davis. Like others in their home winemaking group, the Mulders have kept a family feeling about their small enterprise. They have been joined by their son-in-law Stanley Hall, a former plant engineer with Paul Masson Winery, who handles winery operations. ❖

Estrella River epitomizes what many people think of as a traditional winery. It's an easily understandable unit, a self-contained kingdom of soil and vegetation, winery and winery family.

From its flag-bright entrance off Highway 46 east, you drive through vineyards punctuated by the reds, yellows and pinks of rosebushes. Ultimately you arrive at the Spanish-style winery, whose 50-foot observation tower stands like a lighthouse, overlooking a sea of nodding green vines. The word "sea" is hardly an exaggeration; on its 1,000 acres, Estrella grows nine different varietals. "If we used all the grapes we harvested in a given year, we'd end up with 300,000 cases of wine!" says winemaker Tom Myers. About 50% of Estrella (Spanish for "star") grapes are purchased by other wineries. The reason is simple. Estrella grapes are star performers. To date, every varietal wine made from estate-grown grapes has won an award.

Winery "families" come in different sizes. Estrella's family includes 35 full-time and 150 seasonal workers, but is no less close for that. "Most people have been with us for a long time. When we hire new cellar workers, we even give them a quiz on winemaking — and they have to score 80% to stay on the job," says Sarah Gravelle, public relations manager. "They end up being more conscientious — and getting more out of their jobs."

The Giacobine family founded Estrella in 1972 and continues to

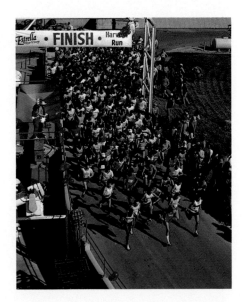

run it as a limited partnership. Major owners are Cliff and Sally Giacobine; three other family members handle everything from vineyard management to finances. Cliff established the winery with his half-brother Gary Eberle, Gary as winemaker, Cliff as administrator. In 1981, Eberle left to found his own winery. He had long been a mentor to Tom Myers, who moved from assistant to head winemaker.

Located about one hour east of Hearst Castle, Estrella River Winery is a popular destination for tour groups and buses that want to combine the romance of San Simeon with the romance of wine. Shaded picnic tables, an entertaining tour, and a fully stocked tasting room make Estrella a draw for more than 50,000 people annually. "We're always trying something new. On holidays, we pair special foods and wines and serve them all day. And we sponsor special events, including our 10K Harvest Run, each fall," says Sarah Gravelle.

A winery this size could get predictable. Estrella, however, continues to sparkle with new

ideas. "We're making an unusual blush wine called Syrah Blanc, and we're getting into sparkling wine production," says Tom Myers. "In two years, we'll be growing by one-third, adding a huge visitor center, gardens, underground champagne cellars — and more." A star now, Estrella may eventually turn into a constellation. ❖

Star trek: miles of vines provide a glorious autumn setting for Estrella's annual 10-kilometer Harvest Run (top left). One of the area's largest wineries, Estrella has a thousand acres under vines, irrigated by a large pond (far left).

Vineyard Visitors

Humans aren't the only ones who are attracted to the vineyards. Many members of the animal kingdom make it their home, or visit regularly. Even animals the size of coyotes. These beautiful bushy-tailed predators often make a circuit of the vineyard, cruising for plump rabbits, snakes and mice who reside in and among the vines. Coyotes — in common with foxes and humans — occasionally like to top off a meal with a cluster of juicy grapes. They also have a taste for rubber. As in drip lines and irrigation hoses.

"At Estrella River Vineyards, we have a problem with coyotes chewing on our drip lines. Basically, it's a drink of water they are after," says Sarah Gravelle of Estrella River.

What do vineyard managers do about coyotes? Most of the time, nothing much. "Oh, we might use shotguns to scare them. But we have far worse critters than coyotes to contend with." ❖

Farview·Farm Vineyard

If prizes were handed out for the loveliest vineyard, Farview Farm would win one, hands down. A few miles west of U.S. 101, you turn left off Highway 46 onto Bethel Road. It curves sweetly past 51 acres of lovely old oaks and luxuriant vines — a roughly equal mix of Zinfandel, Chardonnay and Merlot grapes.

Partners Daniel Roy and John Kozik began planting their vines in 1972. Now at their peak, the vines yield 300 tons per year. "We view ourselves first as a vineyard, second as a winery," says Dan Roy. "Our strategy is to sell prime grapes to other wineries, and then to make a limited quantity of select wine for our label," adds Kozik.

The wines made by these two adoptive Californians include Chardonnay, Merlot, Zinfandel and a white Zin — all made at leased facilities.

Despite its petite size, Farview's markets are far-flung. "Our wines are distributed statewide in restaurants, grocery stores and other outlets and in Japan and British Colombia. The Canadian and the Japanese particularly like our white Zinfandels," says Kozik.

Their wines have won ribbons, but the partners seem more pleased with the public's perception of Farview Farm. "In the early 1970s, we were all very stylistic and made the wines we wanted. Now we are aiming at what the consumers want. Thank God that consumers are gaining more faith in their own taste!" says Dan Roy. ❖

GREAT SHAPES

In the beginning was the Chianti bottle shape: a fat blob with a long narrow neck. Even the bottom was round. Perhaps you're wondering how they ever set the darned things down. They used wooden or metal racks — a system which worked fine until the picnic was invented.

In early times, wines weren't meant to age. Later, winemakers — and glassblowers — gained more skill. A classic winebottle shape began to develop in the Bordeaux district of France. It was a masculine-looking bottle with firm, high shoulders and flat sides, designed to make it easy to store the ageing wine on its side. It became a tradition to use green glass for red wines, clear for whites. In California, you'll also find many of the "blush" wines in Bordeaux-style clear bottles, where their pretty colors of coral, salmon and copper can be seen to best advantage.

While the Bordeaux bottle was taking shape, the winemaking folks in Burgundy, the Rhone district and the Loire Valley were developing their own bottle. As feminine as the Bordeaux is masculine, the Burgundian bottle has a longer neck, more curve to its sides and a fatter bottom. In California and Europe, winemakers generally put their Chardonnay and Pinot Noir in Burgundian bottles. Chardonnays are distinguished by an olive green glass, called "dead leaf green" by the literal French.

While the French were whipping up these bottle shapes, German winemakers were busy trying to one-up them by inventing an even more aristocratic shape. What they came up with was the flute, a beautiful swan-necked bottle in brown glass for Rhine wine, green for Moselle wines. A variety of California white wines use the flute shape, including Gewürtztraminer and Riesling. ❖

HMR
HIDDEN MOUNTAIN RANCH

Deep in the Santa Lucia foothills hides a 25,000-case winery whose logo is an artistic rendering of the terrain. If you didn't know better, you'd swear this was Steinbeck country: indigo sky, tight golden hills, country roads.

At the end of one such road sits HMR winery, surrounded by almonds, grazing land and 65 acres of vines. Now 20 years old, the vineyards struggle up and down steep chalky hillsides in a lovely locale called "an ecological jewel" by wine authority André Tchelistcheff.

Winemaker Chris Johnson adds: "Our vines look like heck because they suffer a bit to grow on these hills. That's what makes the fruit so good." Like other ambitious winemakers, Chris is wrestling with the challenge of making a truly great Pinot Noir. Johnson dabbled at winemaking as he grew up, attending U.C. Davis, then going east to work for Wagner Vineyards in New York. Now he is making Chardonnay, Chenin Blanc, Sauvignon Blanc, Cabernet Sauvignon and Pinot Noir for HMR Estate.

The winery was originally founded by Dr. Stanley Hoffman, who made its wine for a decade. Six miles east of the winery, you'll find the Paso Robles tasting room. Tiny and trim, the white clapboard building offers a bar, wine sales and a few gift items. ❖

Las Tablas Winery

Perched on a thousand-foot-high hill off Las Tablas Road is a winery with a view most San Francisco restaurateurs would kill for. "On a clear day we can see northeast to the Diablo Range," says Della Mertens, who owns Las Tablas with her husband John.

Originally from New York, the Mertens stumbled across a Templeton winery for sale in the 1970s. They ended up changing the name and moving the winery to its panoramic site. A pair of resourceful recyclers, the Mertens paneled their tasting room with wood from the original winery's ancient vats. They plan to have 40 acres under vines eventually.

The Mertens make about 4,000 cases a year of Zinfandel, sweet Muscat, rosé and white wine — all of it sold through the tasting room. "For me, that's the best part: meeting the people who find their way here from all over the world," says Della. The antique-filled tasting room sells local crafts and wine-related gifts.

How do the Mertens view winemaking? On the wall is a quote from Ben Franklin which probably sums it up: "Wine is constant proof that God loves us and loves to see us happy." ❖

Martin Brothers

Artistic sensibility and a love of things Italian: these are the common bonds of the family enterprise called Martin Brothers Winery. At first glance, the winery has an all-American look, housed in the trim grey-and-white buildings of a former dairy and surrounded by vines and grazing land. Then you start taking in details. A door that's a work of art. The Nebbiolo wine labels, which use sketches from da Vinci and Michelangelo. And the Nebbiolo itself: an Italian wine getting its name from the *nebbia* or fog of the Piedmont region. Martin Brothers is currently the only winery to make this red wine classic in quantity.

Besides Nebbiolo, they make Chardonnay, Sauvignon Blanc, Chenin Blanc and Zinfandel. Seven family members work at the winery: brothers Dominic and Tom, sisters Ann and Mary, sister-in-law Patrice, brother-in-law David and father Edward. In the 1930s, Edward worked as a publicist for California's first bonded winery in Cucamonga. "He gave the whole family an education in wine appreciation," says Patrice, who handles marketing with Tom. Dominic went on to study winemaking at U.C. Davis, working at Mirassou and Lambert Bridge Wineries.

In 1981, the family bought its property off Highway 46 east and began putting in vines. Since then, they have become staunch supporters of the local Mozart Festival, doing an annual fund-raiser and a special wine.

A new tasting room is in the works. And by 1990, the Martins hope to be 90% estate bottled. "To utilize our grapes, we plan to grow to 18,000 cases per year," says winemaker Nick Martin. ❖

Warm welcome: from its rosewood and cast bronze doors to its new tasting room, Martin Brothers Winery pleases the eye.

MASTANTUONO

Writers love a guy like Pasquale (Pat) Mastantuono. He's what is known as "good copy:" a pilot, a historian, a big-game hunter and a people-pleaser, always ready with a quip, a wink, another drop of his fine Zinfandel. But the humor belies the substantial side of Pat. More than a winemaker or a raconteur, he is a teacher. Three wineries in his area can be said to owe their existence to him.

For years, Pat, his wife Leona and their two girls lived in Topanga Canyon. By day, Pat designed custom furniture for the likes of Elvis Presley and Sammy Davis, Jr. Other times, he made wine. And he taught others how to do it his way. Most of his "graduates" ended up establishing wineries in this region.

During the Los Angeles years, Pat had the vision of retiring to Paso Robles to make wine. "Twenty-five years ago, I bought grapes from here," he says. Purchasing land was a logical next step.

In 1983, Pat designed and built the large tasting room which stands at the junction of Vineyard Drive and Highway 46 west. Tucked in a grove of massive, moss-clad oaks is a 2-story chateau whose architectural style Pat calls "Early Mastantuono."

Besides a handsome bar made from a huge slab of cedar, the tasting room reveals enough treasures to stock a small museum.

32 Paso Robles Area

Paso Robles Area 33

One of a kind: winemaker Pasquale Mastantuono (non-Italians can call him "Pat Mastan") has left his mark on wine and local architecture alike. Pat calls his traffic-stopping tasting chateau "Early Mastantuono."

Which indeed it is. At the entrance rests a 160-year-old press. In the corner, an old safe holds cold apple juice. Wall cases display antique corkscrews and old tools. Wild boars, swordfish and mule deer trophies stare down in astonishment from the walls.

A tireless magpie, Mastan has collected wine memorabilia for decades. "Some of my best pieces came from an 81-year-old bootlegger from Cucamonga. He was burned out by other bootleggers in 1935, but saved part of his still, some machinery and some wonderful brass lab equipment. I bought all of it in 1973."

Most of the winemaking equipment is at the Willow Creek facility, some miles from the tasting room. "We do have barrel ageing, case storage and a little winery below the tasting room," says Pat.

Pat, whose Italian ancestors include a captain in Garibaldi's army, builds his wine list around Zinfandels. He and Leona are especially proud of their Centennial, a reserve Zinfandel made from 100-year-old vines. "We spend much time getting the choicest grapes. We go through our vineyards three different times, to pick the grapes at their exact moment."

The Mastantuonos make 8,000 cases a year, most of it Zinfandel. Do they plan to grow bigger? Pat's eyebrows shoot up and down. "If this winery gets any bigger," he says, "it will *seriously* interfere with my fishing." ❖

34 Paso Robles Area

MISSION VIEW
VINEYARDS

"Five years — that's what it takes to make a dream come true." Cathy and Terry Peterson sit in their tasting room/kitchen, surveying their 'dream' — 40 acres of healthy vines.

Once you have gotten off Highway 101 and gone one mile southeast along River Road, you spot a mellow, two-story structure, its hexagonal window framed by live oaks. Flowers and rainbow-striped wind-catchers soften the newness of the winery, completed in 1985.

Mission View's creators, the Petersons, met ten years ago. At that time, they were both with United Air Lines — Cathy as flight attendant, Terry as pilot. Cathy has since retired to tackle wine marketing. Terry continues to alternate flying with winemaking.

A gifted amateur who began making wine with Los Angeles friends, Terry has also taken extension courses at U.C. Davis. (One of his mentors, Pat Mastan, makes wine down the road from Mission View.)

Encouraged by the awards Terry was winning and the quality of the Paso Robles grapes they were getting, the Petersons began looking for land in 1978. Two years later, they found it, near San Miguel Arcangel, one of California's most beautiful rural missions. The country surrounding both mission and winery is dramatic. Dry, intensely golden hills flow down to the Salinas River Valley, green and lush.

From the outset, the Petersons wanted an estate program. Planting began in 1981; now their wines are all made from Zinfandel, Sauvignon Blanc, Cabernet Sauvignon, Chardonnay and Muscat Canelli grapes grown on the premises.

New as it is, Mission View has gotten considerable attention. Its Bacchanal Blanc — a white Zinfandel the color of coral — has collected ribbons and writeups. Cathy, whose prowess in marketing has gotten Mission View wines headed for national distribution, enjoys promoting wine. "It has been a real thrill to do California wine promotion in Hawaii, London and other locales," says Terry.

Visitors to Mission View are in for special treatment. Tours and tasting are far from routine. Terry is glad to explain the finer points of the winery, which he also designed. "We make it a point to share with people all the things we've done here," says Cathy. "For instance, we'll take visitors right into our vineyards. We'll show them how to identify the different varietals, how a field press works — we even show them what large versus small quantities of water on the vines can do." Does that kind of attention pay off? "You bet. People are so appreciative, so receptive — and that's our biggest reward." ❖

Paso Robles Area

Old vines, old vats and Old World tradition: these are the hallmarks of Pesenti Winery, which has been making wines near Templeton since 1934. This three-generation family operation was founded by Frank Pesenti. His son Victor, son-in-law Aldo Nerelli and grandson Frank continue the tradition.

Getting there is part of the pleasure. You take winding, scenic Vineyard Drive west off Highway 101. Just when you think it couldn't get any prettier, you come to steep hillsides covered with Pesenti vines — some as much as 62 years old — and the winery itself.

"It's funny — we've found that some of our oldest and simplest equipment continues to be the best thing to do the job," says Frank Nerelli, winemaker since 1970. "These 12,500-gallon redwood tanks, for instance." He points to four giant casks, stained an aromatic burgundy from years of holding wines. "And our fermenters are the same ones my grandfather used."

To harvest its grapes, Pesenti Winery uses a German field crusher called a *mortl*. It may be the only one in use in San Luis Obispo County. "With it, crews can pick nine tons a day and leave the flies, bees and stems out in the field," notes Frank.

The Pesentis and the Nerellis, intertwined through marriage, make wines in the Italian manner. Their 75 acres of Zinfandel and Cabernet Sauvignon grapes are dry farmed. Red wines are made in small batches, with hotter fermentation and lots of hand labor. Frank likes the Italian style of punching the cap down twice a day in the fermenter. The results taste European also.

"Our wines — especially our Zinfandels and our Cabernets — are a little bolder," comments Frank. Among their award winners are the 1983 Zinfandel Ruby and a 1982 late harvest dry Zinfandel. They also make several well-received blush wines plus a complete line of varietals and generic wines — red, white, rosé and sweet dessert. A winemaker like his father and grandfather before him, Frank calls winemaking "the only life I know."

Looking back on the last decade, he remembers 1982 and 1984 as "very good vintage years for us." He is especially proud of his 1982 Cabernet Sauvignon Nouveau, which took a gold medal at the Los Angeles County Fair against a number of Napa Valley wines.

Unlike its new neighbors, Pesenti Winery estalished its niche long ago. "And we're very happy with it," adds Aldo Nerelli. Fifty percent of their wine sales are made through the tasting room, which also stocks food, gift and gourmet items.

Aldo Nerelli sums it up: "Year after year, we make new customers and the old ones keep coming back. We figure we must be doing something right." ❖

Rolling Ridge

"Chardonnay that stresses fruit and elegance. And big deep red wines with long ageing potential." That's how winemaker Cliff Hight describes what he is after.

Rolling Ridge Winery, established in 1983 by owner Alan West, sits on a hill near San Miguel. From its barren slopes you have a panoramic view of the Salinas River Valley and the town of Paso Robles, winking in the distance. To the east brood deeply-furrowed hills, reminiscent of Hemingway's "hills like white elephants." This is a stark, elemental landscape, as empty of people as in mission days.

The winery is a simple facility with a 2,000-square-foot barrel room but no tasting amenities. Visitors are directed to Templeton Corner, where the apple-crisp Chardonnay and the reds of Rolling Ridge are available. Besides Chardonnay, Cliff makes Cabernet Sauvignon, Zinfandel, Petite Sirah, Merlot and Barbera wine.

At Rolling Ridge since its inception, Cliff's involvement with winemaking goes back to 1958. At that time, he learned Old World techniques from a winemaker in Santa Cruz County, later spending three years with Cygnet Cellars in neighboring San Benito County.

With 40 acres under vines and 30 more to be planted, Rolling Ridge plans to expand its line to include a Cabernet Franc. But "keep it small" seems to be the watchword: 5,000 cases a year, marketed by the owner and winemaker directly to premium wine shops throughout Southern California. ❖

ABOUT THE WINERY
East of the Salinas river near Mission San Miguel is our own little Eden — Rolling Ridge Winery. Close at hand lies Jones Ranch, where we grow our Cabernet Sauvignon grapes. This is a landscape of 300-year-old oaks and tawny hills, a valley of blazing summer days and nights tempered by cool breezes from the Salinas River Valley. Our Cabernet Sauvignon grapes prosper here, just as the Mission padres did two centuries ago.

1982
Paso Robles

Cabernet Sauvignon

VINTED & BOTTLED BY ROLLING RIDGE WINERY
SAN MIGUEL, CA • ALC. 13% BY VOLUME • BW 5184

ABOUT THE WINE
This full-bodied wine made from 100% Cabernet Sauvignon grapes should be aged five to ten years. Our region is famous for its viticultural qualities. In it, the grapes regularly experience temperature variances of up to 50 degrees from day to night. This in turn intensifies the already pronounced varietal character and flavor of our grapes.

Aged in oak, this wine possesses an excellent acid finish and alcohol balance. Its refreshing taste will go well with French cuisine and other delicately-flavored dishes.

Paso Robles Area

Santa Lucia Winery

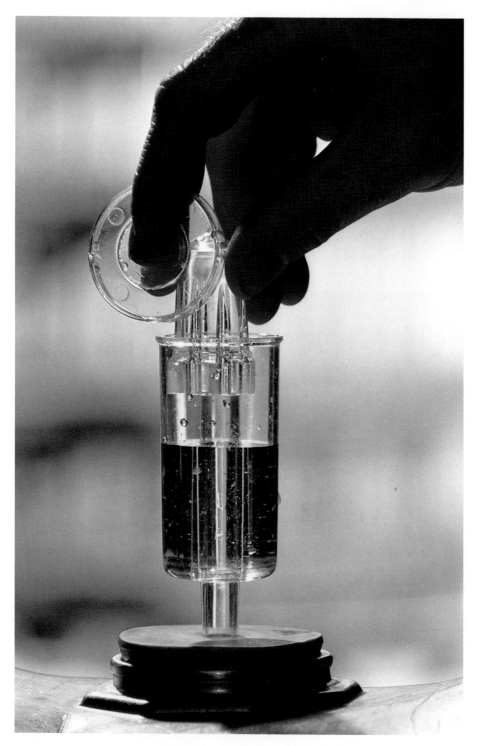

Tools of the trade: on small containers, winemakers like Ken Volk use fermentation locks to keep oxygen out while venting CO_2 gas.

In the spring of 1986, this Templeton winery released its first wine — a 1983 Pinot Noir on the romantic Wild Horse label. Santa Lucia was founded by Ken Volk, who grew up in San Marino, got his degree in fruit science from Cal Poly in San Luis Obispo and learned his skills at several county wineries. In 1981, he bought land and began planting Chardonnay and Cabernet vines the following spring, aiming for an estate program by 1986.

He is a partisan of traditional winemaking: open fermentation of red wines, gravity racking and transfer of the wine. "I believe in treating the wines as gently as I can," he says. Ken Volk makes Merlot, Pinot Noir, Cabernet Sauvignon and Chardonnay.

Headed for a 5,000-case maximum, Ken markets his wines through mail order, local distributors and the tasting room at nearby Templeton Corner.

Future plans? "With my wife, I eventually intend to open a restaurant and winery somewhere along the coast — primarily to take advantage of the coastal traffic to and from Hearst Castle." ❖

Small wineries present a dilemma to the potential visitor-taster. They invite exploration, yet are often too limited — in size or staff — to permit tasting or tours. Templeton Corner has come up with a solution to please visitors and wineries. Owners George and Ann Nagano have combined a gourmet delicatessen with a tasting room which promotes the wines of more than 15 small wineries.

Templeton Corner is located in the ranching village of Templeton, as western as a slow drawl. The store is a pleasant, airy place, graced by huge oil paintings and interesting winery photos and clippings. You can choose to sit on the shady patio or in the air-conditioned interior.

George and his staff are eager to help visitors taste and compare local wines. "The wineries we represent put a lot of T.L.C. into their wines — you get a fine sense that they are handcrafted, premium products," says George. "Here, you have a unique opportunity to try nearly 30 wines from a 3-county area." To taste, the Naganos charge a small fee which is required by law.

Besides wines by the glass or bottle, the Corner has tempting delicacies: local cheeses, sandwiches, desserts and daily specials. They gladly fix picnic lunches also. Open daily til 5 p.m., Templeton Corner's easy access and long hours make it a don't-miss proposition for wine lovers. ❖

At ease: the Naganos (pictured right) provide helpful hints and a relaxed atmosphere for comparing local wines.

Tobias

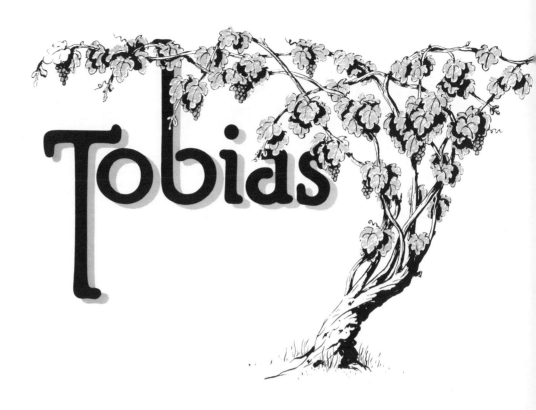

Not many children have a legacy like Tobias and Jed Wheeler. Tobias, the oldest son, has a winery named after him. His brother has been immortalized with a robust jug wine called "Jed's Big Red."

The tiniest winery in San Luis Obispo County, Tobias is the creation of Pat Wheeler. A tool and diemaker by trade, Pat got involved with home winemaking through a Yugoslav fisherman turned winemaker. That encounter sparked Pat's interest, who went on to study winemaking with Pat Mastan and the Los Angeles Home Winemakers Club. Pat also took courses at U.C. Davis and Cal Poly, San Luis Obispo. Like Wheeler, Pat's partner Doug Beckett is a Southern California transplant.

Tobias specializes in Petite Sirah and Zinfandel wines. Most of the grapes come from the Dusi, Jones and Radike Ranches in Templeton and San Miguel. In 1980, Tobias' first commercially crushed Zinfandel took gold medals at both the Santa Barbara and San Luis Obispo County Fairs.

Tobias Vineyards makes big, heavy wines with the feel of the frontier about them. To sample their honest, rough-hewn quality, visitors can inquire at Templeton Corner, (see opposite page) 6th and Main in Templeton, and at the Cambria General Store. Located at 850 Main in Cambria, the latter offers a limited number of wines to taste on a daily basis, and often features local wines. ❖

TONIO CONTI

Like a fine champagne, Tonio Conti is already making a splash. The first sparkling wine venture to be launched in this region, Conti is headed by winemaker John Munch and ten Swiss investors.

In early 1986, Conti's first 1,700 cases of Blanc de Blancs, made from 1982 harvest Chardonnay grapes, were released to compliments all around. "We're extremely excited about the possibilities here," says Munch. "We've already competed against French and Napa Valley Blanc de Blancs and have come out very well. This microclimate in the Paso Robles appellation is giving us ideal fruit for *méthode champenoise* wines. And for other wines too."

For the time being, Tonio Conti leases facilities at Estrella River Winery. "We have a nice synergistic relationship," notes John. "We have use of Estrella's crush equipment. In turn, they have use of our specialized sparkling wine equipment. Each of us handles all aspects of our own production, but by sharing the machinery we both profit."

"Our goal is to reach 20,000 cases a year," continues Munch. "We're going about it slowly, gently. Buying our own facilities, building a tasting room, planting vineyards — this will occupy us over the next six years." About 200 acres are being planted in Chardonnay, Pinot Noir and Pinot Blanc grapes.

The Conti label conveys the classic feeling Munch and his partners are trying to get across. Designed by Wesley Poole, it combines tradition with a touch of flair — a design as clean as a dove's wing. ❖

Twin Hills Ranch

"Wine doesn't just go with food — it *is* a food. A good food. It adds one more dimension to a great meal." That's the philosophy of Jim Lockshaw, Twin Hills owner, winemaker, gourmet cook and food enthusiast.

Twin Hills, established in 1983, has a graceful tasting room that combines Lockshaw's enthusiasm for good wine and food. You spot it four miles out of Paso Robles along Nacimiento Lake Drive. Spacious, adorned with arbors, country French in style, the tasting room has outdoor tables, a tasting bar and a picnic area. Besides sampling Twin Hills wines, you can nibble light foods, buy local agricultural products from almonds to smoked meats — and sometimes taste cheeses made by Lockshaw himself.

Jim brings his own special philosophy to bear on the winemaking process also. "I don't know anyone else who pursues our 'natural wine' methodology. It takes a lot of work. We use no herbicides, no artificial fertilizers. And before we crush, we actually wash our grapes in half-ton lots," says Jim. The award ribbons that already hang in Lockshaw's winery validate the soundness of this approach.

Made in a light, drinkable style, his wines are produced from 43 acres of estate-grown grapes. The line includes Chardonnay,

Ground floor: winemaker Jim Lockshaw (right) looks over the plans for his beautifully realized tasting room.

Chenin Blanc, Zinfandel, Zin Rosé, white Zin and a small amount of Cabernet Sauvignon.

"I'm experimenting with a Spanish-style sherry too," notes Lockshaw. "By 1988, we should know how it's going to come out." Sales of Twin Hills wines are already at the 15,000 case per year mark, with the ultimate goal being twice that.

Twin Hills gets its name from two graceful hills, cross-hatched with almond trees and vines, where the winery itself lies. How did an Orange County businessman end up in this hidden corner of California? Jim responds: "We had been looking around for some time. When we came across this property, my oldest son Curtis said, 'This place *is* what California is supposed to be.' And he was right." ❖

WATSON

"Some people have yachts. This is our yacht," says Bryan Watson, pointing to his winery.

On the crest of a hill near Paso Robles live the Watsons — Bryan, wife Jennifer, son Mark, three dogs, two cats, two fish and a newt. Southern Californians who divide their time between the cultural attractions of Santa Barbara and the rural satisfactions of Paso, the Watsons exemplify the "best of both worlds" approach that many families are after.

On their liter-sized estate, they have planted ten acres of Riesling and Pinot Noir. That production, plus purchased grapes, lets them make about a thousand cases a year. The wines include Pinot Noir, Johannisberg Riesling, Chardonnay, and a Chenin Blanc as delicate as the almond trees on the land.

Their first harvest in 1982 was memorable. "We brought 20 friends to pick," recalls Bryan. "It was great fun — for the first hour. After that, we had to get new friends."

The family was drawn to the area by an ad that read 'restorable almond orchard.' "When we found that it was part of the old Ignace Paderewski Ranch, we knew that grapes would do well," says Bryan. With the help of rancher Francis Nelson, they put in vines.

The Watsons intend to make 5,000 cases a year, marketing mail order and in select outlets. Area visitors can sample their wines at Templeton Corner.

Besides the pleasure of making what Bryan calls "something noble," the Watsons have reaped other benefits. Says Jennifer: "This venture has brought us together in a family effort. I've never heard so much laughter." Their label bears a family crest: "I owe everything to God and country." It could just as easily read: "Laughter makes good wine." ❖

YORK MOUNTAIN

In anyone's book of superlatives, York Mountain Winery would rate two entries. Established in 1882, it's the oldest continuously operating winery in three local counties. And it's the only winery located in the York Mountain appellation, honoring the special character of the grapes grown in this small viticultural area.

But York Mountain is more than statistics. To reach it, you climb 1,500 feet up picturesque York Mountain road from Highway 46 west. There, you are greeted by the winery's welcoming façade, made of circa-1880 bricks. Huge beams, retrieved from the ocean pier nine miles west at Cambria, grace the interior. Machinery, 100-year-old casks and memorabilia from over a century of winemaking are on display.

Three generations of Yorks preceded the Goldmans, who now operate the winery. In 1882, Andrew York bought the land and planted grapevines. World-famous statesman and pianist Ignace Paderewski, who lived on a neighboring vineyard, had his famous Zinfandel made at York Mountain. York's descendants continued the tradition. In 1970, veteran enologist Max Goldman bought this secluded property. "My father had faith in this area," recalls son Steve, winemaker since 1970. On the Wine Institute's Board of Directors and a past president of the American Society of Enologists, Max shared his winemaking knowledge with his college graduate son. Other family members are now involved, including daughter Suzanne, who manages the tasting room.

The winery makes six varietals and three generics, with a port and sherry to be released in late 1986.

Still famous for its Zinfandels, York Mountain has taken awards in other categories as well. Steve is proudest of the 1980 Pinot Noir, which took medals in four separate competitions. Most of York

Mountain's wine is sold through its tasting room.

At one time in the last century, the winery was called Ascension. The Goldmans are reviving that name on a new label, to designate the wines made from grapes of the York Mountain appellation. Explains Steve: "We want to promote our appellation and, as much as possible, make our wines from its grapes."

Besides the opportunity to taste its wines, people will continue to view York Mountain Winery as a special outing. It is that kind of place: a vivid link with the past, a friendly landmark of the present ❖

San Luis Obispo
AREA

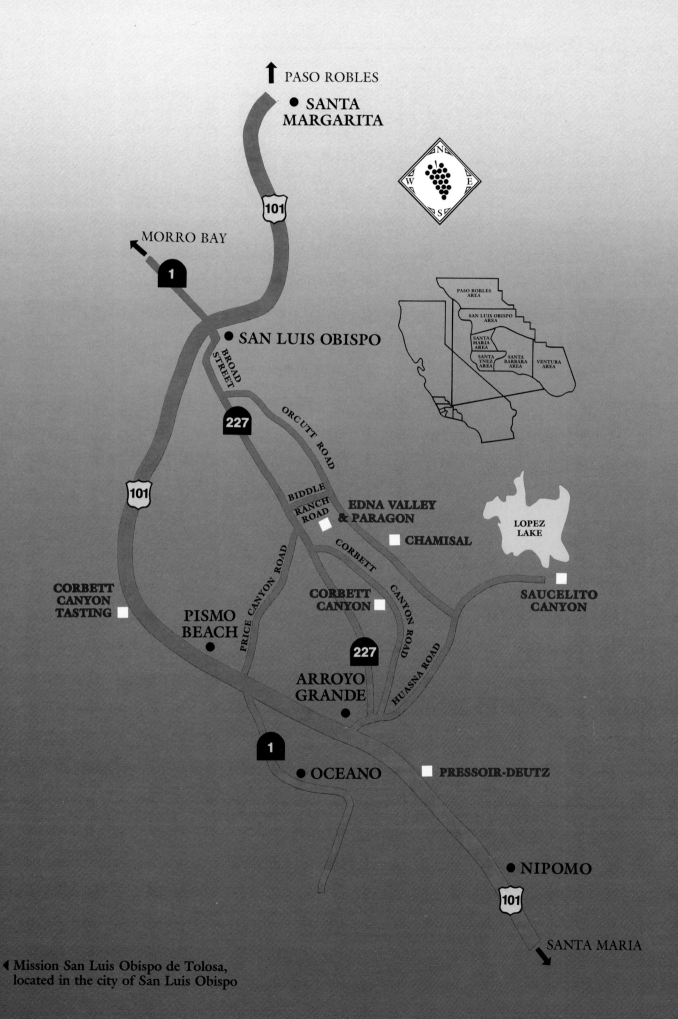

◀ Mission San Luis Obispo de Tolosa, located in the city of San Luis Obispo

50 San Luis Obispo Area

Chamisal Vineyard

San Luis Obispo Area 51

Take a Le Montrachet clone of Chardonnay grape; add the soil and climate of Edna Valley; gently stir in the talents of winemaker Scott Boyd. The result is a prize-winning Chardonnay that has been applauded since its first release.

The idea behind Chamisal began in the 1960s, when restaurateur Norman Goss noticed the trend from red to white wines among his clientele. Acting on his feeling that Chardonnay would become California's "hot ticket," Goss bought a piece of the old Rancho Bolsa de Chamisal and planted 57 acres of vines. Thirty years earlier, Goss and his family had attended a lunch given by pianist Ignace Paderewski, who served a memorable Zinfandel from his own vineyard near San Luis Obispo. That memory helped determine Goss's choice of Edna Valley.

Chamisal became a family affair. Son Tom studied viticulture and took over the vineyards. Daughter Allyn prepared a marketing program, and Scott Boyd became winemaker. Boyd, with degrees from Cal Poly and U.C. Davis, had worked at Roudon-Smith Vineyards.

Located off Orcutt Road south of San Luis Obispo, Chamisal occupies a simple and charming site. The 5,000-case winery is styled after the great chateaux of France, growing all its own grapes and making but one wine a year. Originally, Chamisal experimented with Sauvignon Blanc and Cabernet, "but Chardonnay has become our calling card," as Scott puts it.

The winery has an intimate patio and tasting room overlooking the vines. Barbecue pits, plantings and a fence for wind protection make the area attractive to individuals or groups.

Intent on winemaking though he is, Scott Boyd gives wine second place in his priorities. "My family relationships — especially with my children Cam and Sutter — are the most important things in my life. When I think about wine, I don't picture some romantic vision. Instead, I see a family like ours around a dinner table, drinking wine, enjoying homegrown food, celebrating the bounty of the earth and the congeniality of the moment." ❖

CORBETT CANYON
V I N E Y A R D S

Just south of San Luis Obispo, a spectacular series of volcanic peaks ends in a round exclamation point called Islay Hill. Beyond Islay lies Edna Valley, a landscape in miniature. Freckled with the smallest of hills, cut with tiny canyons, Edna Valley has two superlatives to boast about. One is the quality of its grapes. The other is Corbett Canyon, a handsome mission-style winery headed for

San Luis Obispo Area

"Coming from an Amador County winemaking background, I was a typical Northern California chauvinist. My attitude changed very quickly once I began working with central coast growers. Some of the finest grapes I have ever made wine from are grown in this region."

— Cary Gott, Corbett Canyon winemaker

eventual production of one million gallons of wine annually.

When the winery was purchased in 1981 by Glenmore Distilleries, it underwent a name change, a staff change and a philosophy reversal. Such turnabouts don't come quickly — or cheaply. Under the guidance of winemaker and President Cary Gott, Corbett Canyon has spent three years and $2 million to achieve its goals.

"Our major thrust was to create three distinct lines of wine. Our Coastal Classic line, marketed in 1-liter bottles unique to us, is already very successful," says Cary. "Our varietal wines reached the market in 1984, and in 1986 we released our Winemaker's Reserve lots." From a three-generation winemaking family, Cary studied at U.C. Davis and served apprenticeships at Inglenook and Sterling Vineyards. In 1973, he and his wife began Monteviña Winery, whose wines established Cary as an outstanding winemaker.

To reach Corbett Canyon, you take Highway 227 out of San Luis Obispo. From 227, you make a hairpin turn onto Corbett Canyon Road, named for a blacksmith who settled these parts. The winery itself sits on a hill, surrounded by countryside as rural as the California of one hundred years ago.

The large rambling building exudes friendliness, as does the staff. "This is a place where people want to come to work," comments Cary Gott. "There's something to be learned here."

Large as it is, Corbett Canyon buys all of its grapes. The philosophy has been to use the

finest grapes from noted vineyards in San Luis Obispo and Santa Barbara Counties. Among them are: Paragon, Santa Maria Hills, Tepusquet, Rancho Sisquoc and Bien Nacido Vineyards. Being in the midst of premium vineyards without owning them has given the winery flexibility. "This way, we've invested in things like a new bottling line, new cooperage and pressing equipment," says Gott.

Visitors have their choice of tasting rooms — one at the winery, another located at Shell Beach along Highway 101. Another attraction is the winery's 3-story dejuicer — a vast metallic giant right out of *War of the Worlds*.

Besides money, Corbett Canyon has spent time and energy building its new identity. Its public relations calendar includes numerous imaginative events, from the popular Christmas Craft Fairs to the annual Mozart Festival.

Besides the Pacific states, Corbett Canyon is carrying its moderately priced wines to the Midwest. Cary Gott says, "We see the rest of the U.S. as our frontier. As the market grows, we plan to grow, and get better as we grow." ❖

Good neighbors: known for lively events like the annual Grape Run and one-time spectaculars like the Renaissance Faire (above), Corbett Canyon also contributes to the area's economic well-being through grape purchases. Paragon Vineyards (preceding pages) is a major supplier.

Pressoir-Deutz Winery

On the steep limestone hillsides around Picacho Peak near Arroyo Grande, 150 acres of grapes are growing. Some of the vines show lush foliage. But most are sparse, shy-bearing varietals used to make fine champagne: Pinot Noir, Pinot Blanc, Pinot Meunier and Chardonnay.

Like their vines, the people at Pressoir-Deutz work at a measured pace. "We're growing the way I like to — very slowly," says winemaker Harold Osborne. "We're not after immediate impact. Our aim is to make sparkling

San Luis Obispo Area

Field work: training young vines is one of the ongoing jobs in the hillside vineyards of Pressoir-Deutz. The winery lies just south of Picacho Peak, a landmark along U.S. 101.

wines with character and longevity."

Pressoir-Deutz, a partnership owned by five Frenchmen, is totally committed to making *méthode champenoise* sparkling wines in the French way. Visiting the winery, you quickly get a sense of this. Dominating the crush room is a 4.4-ton traditional champagne basket press — the only one of its kind in the U.S. The vast room where riddling takes place is equally impressive. You see row upon row of tilted bottles, each of which must be given 25 careful turns (⅛ turn a day) to move sediment into the bottle necks. All of this is hand labor of the most delicate kind.

"Making good Champagne-style sparkling wine is a long process," agrees Osborne. "First, you make a sound base wine. Then you give it champagne character through a second fermentation in the bottle, followed by two years' ageing in contact with yeast sediment and other steps. That's at least three years of work."

A veteran of Fresno State and U.C. Davis, Osborne worked for eight years at Schramsberg Champagne Cellars in Napa and

has spent additional years studying the Australian and French wine industries. What brought him here? "I was attracted by the fact that André Lallier, President and active partner in this venture, comes from a champagne background dating back to the 1830s. And by the fact that the vineyard site is only four miles from the ocean. This marine influence gives us a long, cool growing season."

Occupying buildings over 25,000 square feet in extent, the Pressoir-Deutz operation has much to offer the visitor interested in the champagne process. It might be wise to call ahead for dates to see dramatic processes such as *dégorgement*. A large handsome tasting room makes a pleasant finale to a tour. However, champagnes made on premises will of necessity be scanty until the winery reaches full production and national distribution in 1990. ❖

Second time around: winemaker Harold Osborne checks out the progress of secondary fermentation in the bottles destined to become méthode champenoise sparkling wines.

Vineyard Visitors

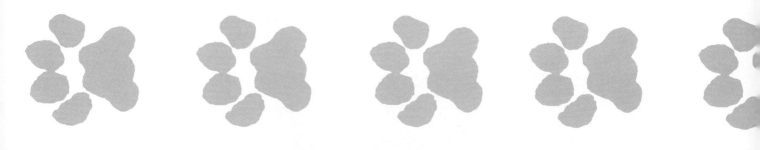

A few grape growers get occasional visits from large predators, such as mountain lions and bobcats. When a mountain lion is in the vineyard, deer stay out. Next to birds, deer are the visitors that grape growers like least. Deer love to nibble the leaves of young grapevines. They've also been known to take their share of ripe grapes.

To keep deer out, it is often necessary to resort to expensive, six-foot-high fencing. "Most of the time, deer graze the outer edges of the vineyards," says Ron Ortega of Old Creek Ranch Winery. "By letting our dogs out at night, we scare most of them off."

Other vineyardists try to repel deer by using items whose odor is obnoxious to the animals. Fur balls of human hair and chips of deodorant soap seem to be especially odious to deer. Perhaps the best deer-discourager of all? Mountain lion dung. ❖

Edna Valley Vineyard

In California, the relationships between vineyards and wineries can get as complex as the wines. Edna Valley is a good example. It's a winery — and a petite vineyard — owned by another, much larger local vineyard named Paragon and a non-local winery named Chalone. If that weren't enough, since 1983 Edna Valley has leased part of its own facilities to a brace of winemakers named Claiborne and Churchill to make their own Gewürztraminer and other wines.

How does all this work out? "Being linked with Paragon, we get the very best grapes available. And Chalone manages our marketing for us. We're left with the most enjoyable part — making the wine," smiles Gary Mosby, winemaker since Edna Valley's inception in 1980. A U.C. Davis grad, Gary has also worked for Sterling, Almaden, Chalone and his own parents' winery, Vega Vineyards.

Edna Valley Vineyard concentrates on premium Chardonnay and Pinot Noir, both made with traditional Burgundian techniques. "However, state health regs don't allow us to crush grapes with human feet. So we've

imitated tradition as best we can with a size-14 mechanical foot clad in a stainless steel tennis shoe," says Gary. Despite this amusing touch, Edna Valley is a serious winery which considers the strong public response to its wines as "the best reward we could have."

Edna Valley has its own underground cellar — one of the few local wineries to possess one. All of its wines undergo ageing in wood for 6-18 months.

Originally a garbanzo-bean farm, the Edna Valley property was planted in vines in 1972. "The owners soon saw they had a winner because the soil was so full of calcium. It ties up soil nutrients, forcing the vines to put all their energy into the fruit," explains Mosby.

In the 35,000-case-per-year range, Edna Valley sells its wines through a large mailing list and through restaurant and retail outlets in 39 states and several foreign countries. The winery offers tours Wednesday through Sunday, and picnickers are welcome to use the picnic area, located in the picturesque midsection of Edna Valley. ❖

Wind and water: vines from Edna Valley and Paragon Vineyards have the advantage of drip irrigation (left) and windmills, which modify air temperatures.

SAUCELITO CANYON

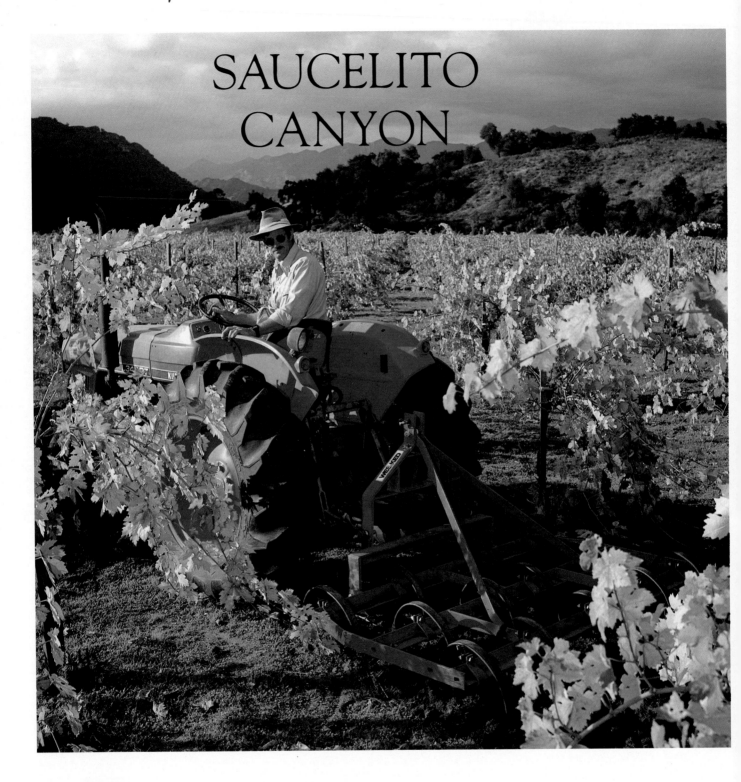

Hidden in the Santa Lucia hills southeast of San Luis Obispo and Arroyo Grande, Saucelito Canyon occupies a 320-acre homestead that was the site of one of the earliest commercial vineyards in the area.

Rugged, beautiful, isolated enough to need a generator for electricity, Saucelito Canyon is the family project of Bill and Nancy Greenough and their three children.

"We've been here a dozen years now. We chose it partly because the old vineyard showed it was the right place to grow grapes," recalls Bill. "It was homesteaded in 1878 by Henry

Ditmus, whose grapes came to have quite a reputation."

The vines were long neglected when Bill and Nancy bought the place, named *Saucelito* for the willows that fringe it. Since then, they have built a house and winery, restored the vineyard, made new plantings and put half a dozen grape harvests behind them. They now make Zinfandel, white Zinfandel and Cabernet Sauvignon. Even their white Zin is barrel fermented. "It gives the wine more complexity — it is also a case of necessity because we lack refrigeration to cool-ferment the wine," says Bill.

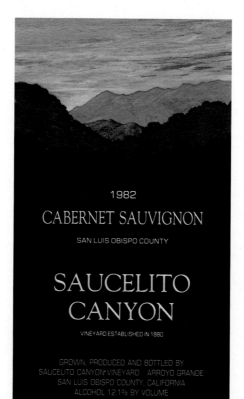

Saucelito now grows 100% of the grapes it needs. "We produce about 2,000 cases a year," says Nancy, who juggles bookkeeping, sales and tastings. "We're probably typical of smaller wineries — we are just now breaking even."

Bill adds: "It's an intellectual challenge to see the winery succeed as a business. But the rewarding thing is to see the vineyard succeed. In Europe, the great growths come from a place — not necessarily a winemaker. Saucelito Canyon wine is beginning to announce its origins." ❖

All grapes are not created equal. There are table grapes, raisin grapes and grapes whose destiny it is to end up as the other half of a peanut-butter-and.

Then there are the superstars: the wine grapes. In Europe, you know where you stand with wine grapes. By law, their wines are identified by geographic region — in some cases, right down to the vineyard the grapes came from. No such luck in California. Our wines can be identified in three different ways. First, by the style in which they are made — Burgundy, Chablis, etc. Known as generics, these wines can be made from a variety of grapes. Second, wine can be identified by a proprietary (invented) name, such as Green Hungarian. Third are the varietal wines, the royalty of California grapes.

To be called "Zinfandel," "Cabernet Sauvignon" or "Pinot Noir," for instance, the wine in the bottle must be made from 75% of that grape varietal. Most of the wineries in this book make varietal wines.

Each varietal represents a specific type of grape that reproduces true to its variety. Besides having clusters of a typical color, shape and aroma, the grape when turned into wine has a predictable signature, which is called its "varietal character."

Confused? Never mind. So is almost everyone else. All the more reason to go wine-tasting — to find out precisely what you do like. And don't like. And in the process, to see and taste the beautiful differences that characterize the wines and grapes of California's coastal heart. ❖

VIVE LA DIFFERENCE

Santa Maria
AREA

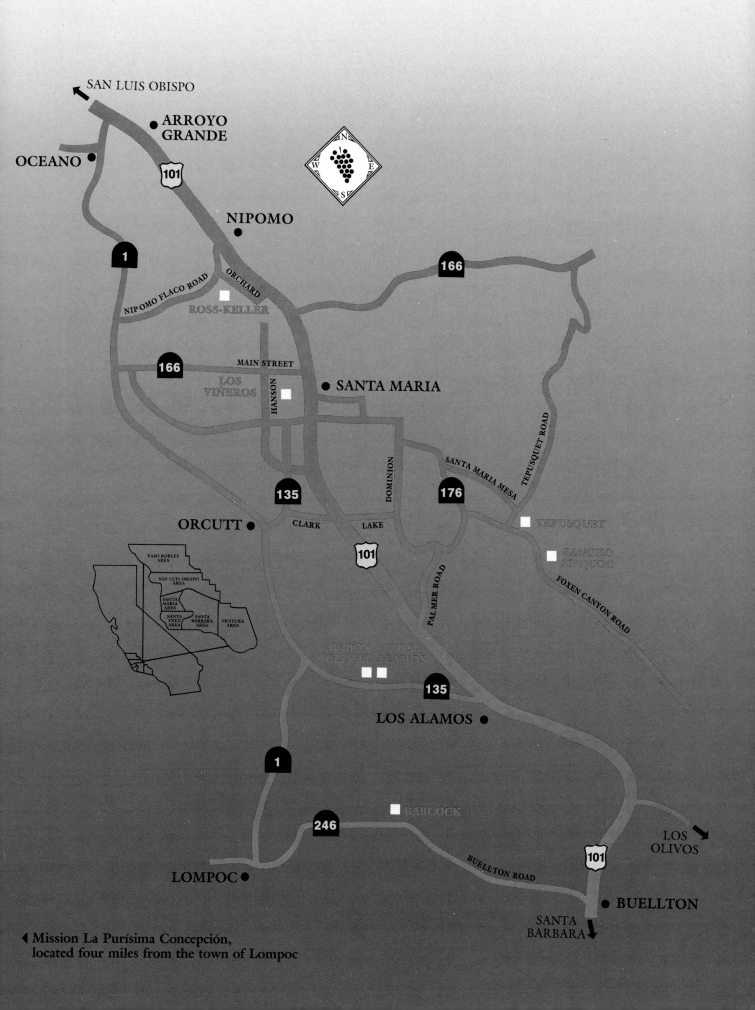

◀ Mission La Purísima Concepción, located four miles from the town of Lompoc

Au Bon Climat

Clearly hand-crafted — that's the message transmitted by Au Bon Climat wines, made since 1982 by Adam Tolmach and Jim Clendenen. One piece of evidence is the triangular label — a special shape which requires meticulous hand labeling. "Our label says that we never intend to get big enough for mass production," says Adam. Tolmach studied viticulture and winemaking at U.C. Davis. After graduation, he went to work for Zaca Mesa Winery. There he met his future partner, who had rejected a law career in favor of wine and had apprenticed as cellarmaster. Eventually the pair decided to make their own wines. "In 1981, we worked the harvest in France and visited 20 Burgundian wineries," says Jim. "That taught us so much."

Each year, the partners make about 3,500 cases of Pinot Noir, Chardonnay and a Pinot Noir-Chardonnay blush wine, using grapes from Los Alamos Vineyards.

Taking its name from the French for a well-situated vineyard, Au Bon Climat wants to position itself as a modestly financed, high-quality alternative to the more lavish wineries in the area. Notes Jim: "People try to peg us as 'French purists.' True, we do use certain methods used in Burgundy. But others do also. What we make is a California wine with European elegance and style." ❖

Hand craft: winemakers Adam Tolmach (pictured) and Jim Clendenen do it all, including hand labeling their wines.

Babcock
VINEYARDS

Like people, wineries don't always fall into neat categories. Babcock is a good example: a family enterprise that seems geographically aligned with Lompoc and the Santa Maria Valley, yet whose grapes enjoy the cool northwestern edge of the Santa Ynez Valley microclimate.

Bonded and built in 1984 ("20 minutes before the first grapes came in!"), Babcock Vineyards has shown that it doesn't intend to be neatly categorized. One of the first wines made from its 40 acres of white varietal grapes was called Le Privilège, a blend of Chenin Blanc and other premium whites. The idea for Le Privilège comes from the French tradition giving landowners the right to make wine from their own grapes.

Walt and Mona Babcock's involvement with wines began 15 years ago, when they opened a seafood restaurant in Seal Beach. In 1979, the couple and their children, Bryan and Brenda, bought this 110-acre parcel and began planting vines. By 1983, their grapes were being used — and praised — by local winemakers. "That was when the family took the plunge and began to build the winery," says Dave Heiber, who makes the wine with Bryan Babcock. Now making Gewürztraminer, Sauvignon Blanc, Johannisberg Riesling, Chardonnay, Pinot Noir and a blush called Le Rouge, the winemakers intend to produce upwards of 5,000 cases a year.

Babcock Vineyards sits amid the famous flower fields of Lompoc. From the winery's vantage point, you gaze out over sweet-scented bands of white, purple, gold and orange blossoms. An amiable, barnlike building, the winery houses a small tasting room which sells wines and two kinds of apples in season.

Youthful as they are, Babcock wines are garnering attention, especially the Gewürztraminer and Le Privilège wines. Dave Heiber counts himself fortunate to work here. "To get a chance like this — fresh out of college — to work with fruit like we're getting. Now that's a *real* 'le privilège'." ❖

Los Alamos Vineyards

If the Gray Panthers had a recruitment poster, Mary Vigoroso would be on it. Winemaker for more than a decade, Mary is a bright-eyed 72-year-old with a talent for making conversation and Cabernet Sauvignon.

"Oh, I've made Chardonnay, Pinot Noir, Zinfandel and Riesling, but my main love is Cabernet," says Mary. "I learned from my grandfather Cosmo, who had a winery near Rome. And his father, and his father before him." Mary's father Salvatore also made wine; Mary still cherishes three bottles of his Cabernet. "They're a legacy for my grandchildren Laura and Mark."

Always involved with family wine, Mary never planned to be a commercial winemaker, much less as a widow of 62. "However, my daughter Dona and son-in-law Sam Hale bought this ranch, planted 350 acres of grapes to sell to large wineries and then decided to start a small winery," recalls Mary. "I offered to help out."

Over the years, the winery has become a one-woman operation. Mary immerses herself in every facet of it. "The first few years, I even loaded up my yellow Volkswagen and marketed the wine," says Mary. Most of the winery's output is sold through the tasting room and at outlets such as the Santa Maria Inn and Trumps restaurant in Los Angeles.

V for vigorous: septuagenarian winemaker Mary Vigoroso makes mellow Cabernet Sauvignon at Los Alamos.

The winery building itself is a minimalist rectangle. Although there is nothing much to see, Mary does give visitors a look around. In her tasting corner, she can make an occasion out of a glass of red wine served on a linoleum-covered table.

And how do visitors react to Mary's combination of velvet-smooth Cabernet and Italian mothering? "They come as visitors — they go away friends," says Mary. Typical of the messages from new friends is a poem left by Craig Meyers, which reads in part:

I have a grandmother like you, Mary
She too had a father
from the old country
and is lined,
and loves honest, hearty things.
She can grow things,
believes in folk medicines
and offers, like your wine,
a personality to chew on.
I have a grandmother like you, Mary
She, too, is. And no excuses.

Another visitor, briefer but no less appreciative, sends a postcard: "Bravo, Mary, bravo!!" ❖

TO YOUR HEALTH

For millenia, wine has been used as medicine, as antiseptic — even as magic potion. Take, for instance, this prescription popular in Greek times:

For the conception of beautiful and virtuous children — mix ground pine nuts, assorted fruits, honey, myrrh, saffron, egg yolk, milk and palm wine.

This mixture, concocted by the physician Democritus, was just one of many uses to which wine was put:

- 2,500 years before Christ, wine was worshipped as a Vedic god for its medicinal properties by the Aryans of India. The Hindus later used it as an anesthetic for surgery.

- Egyptian medical papyri, Sumerian clay tablets and the Old Testament all swore by wine, variously used in salves, mixed with oil and balsam as an antiseptic and as a cooling agent for fevers.

- Galen, who acted as physician to Roman gladiators, noted that red wine on their dressings kept wounds from putrefying.

- Generals from Cyrus the Great to Napoleon issued wine to their troops — not for morale, but to prevent typhoid, cholera and dysentery.

The amazing thing is, wine does live up to most of the claims made for it. Modern scientists were flabbergasted to find that wine actually kills 99% of all typhoid and cholera bacilli in test cultures. Small wonder that, through the ages, the most popular phrase for toasting has been:

To your health!

Los Viñeros

Viñeros is a Spanish word that means grape growers, an appropriate name indeed for this Santa Maria winery owned by eight local *viñeros*. Begun in 1980, Los Viñeros is the joint venture of Bob Woods, Uriel Nielson, George Ott, Eric Caldwell, Boyd Bettencourt, Bill and Dean Davidge and Howard and Charlotte Young. Woods and Nielson alone have two decades apiece as grape growers in the area. Now retired from farming, Uriel grew the first local grapes sold to Christian Brothers back in the early 1960s.

How did eight people manage to agree on all the decisions necessary to develop a coherent winery style? "We were very lucky in our first winemaker, Kurt Lorenzi," says Uriel. "He set the pace and we just followed his lead." Lorenzi, a winemaker and consultant of some stature in this and other parts of California, has since moved on. The current winemaker is Bill Spencer, who had worked with Lorenzi as his assistant at Los Viñeros. Spencer applauds the Los Viñeros way of doing things. "I really like our philosophy of low-temperature fermentation," says Bill. "It gives me a good handle on things." Bill makes about 12,000 cases a year of Pinot Noir, Cabernet Sauvignon, Sauvignon Blanc, Chardonnay, Gewürztraminer and a couple of blush wines — Blanc of Cabernet and Blanc of Pinot Noir. The winery also does quite a bit of custom crushing for other labels.

Barrel thief: like all winemakers, Bill Spencer regularly tastes the wines ageing in cooperage at Los Viñeros.

Santa Maria Area

Like other wineries, Los Viñeros has a tasting-room wall full of ribbons. In 1985, it received an unusual honor: the California Historical Society selected the 1983 Chardonnay for a special limited edition, sold only by subscription. The label depicts a graceful rendering of Bierstadt's painting of Yosemite Gorge. Speaking of labels: in the race for shelf attention, the Los Viñeros logo stands out. Like the Spanish name it bears, the Sebastian Titus-designed logo conveys the color and aristocratic feel of Spain.

In contrast to its elegant label, Los Viñeros has its facility in a decidedly industrial part of Santa Maria. To find Hanson Way, you take Stowell Road west past the railroad tracks and turn right at the city limits. An attractive tasting room fronts the warehouselike winery, where you can taste at the U-shaped bar after looking around. ❖

> "All of us were grape growers first. We saw the winery as a means to take care of our crops."
>
> — Uriel Nielson,
> one of eight partners at Los Viñeros

Rancho Sisquoc

Rancho Sisquoc makes several wines that are unusual for this part of California, including a silky, much-praised Franken Riesling. But getting *to* this rural winery is as much fun as tasting once there.

The prettiest approach is from the north. You exit Highway 101 at Betteravia Road, which turns into the lush green curves of Highway 176 and Foxen Canyon Road. Presently you spot the white spires of San Ramon chapel, built in 1875 and standing like a beacon at the entrance to Rancho Sisquoc.

The winery is small and picturesque, producing about 3,000 cases a year of Johannisberg Riesling, Franken Riesling, Sauvignon Blanc, Chardonnay, Cabernet Blanc, Merlot and Cabernet Sauvignon. "We're really grape growers first, winemakers second," explains ranch manager Harold Pfeiffer. The 36,000-acre ranch, owned by the James Flood family of San Francisco, has 215 acres devoted to grapes. Ninety percent are sold to other wineries. The vineyards run up hill, down dale and along the sometimes-rambunctious Sisquoc River. Manager for 22 years, Pfeiffer is a Princeton man who came west to work and was hired by the Floods to develop the ranch. "We were among the first to plant grapes

around here, largely because several Napa wineries had indicated interest." In 1974, Geyser Peak made its Cabernet Sauvignon from Rancho Sisquoc grapes — the first Santa Maria Valley designation on a North Coast wine.

As the man who put in the vineyards, the irrigation system and the winery, Harold Pfeiffer knows about all there is to know about this terrain. "Take our Franken Riesling — very seldom grown in California because it's considered an 'inferior' grape. But if you grow it in a nice cool climate and leave a little sweetness in it, you end up with a lovely wine," says Harold.

Working with a succession of young winemakers, Pfeiffer has provided continuity for Rancho Sisquoc. "What we're after is a light, elegant wine," he says. And there's no better place to enjoy them than at the tasting room, surrounded by oaks and pecans, grape arbors and tranquil picnic areas. Visitors are encouraged to bring picnics. ❖

ROSS-KELLER

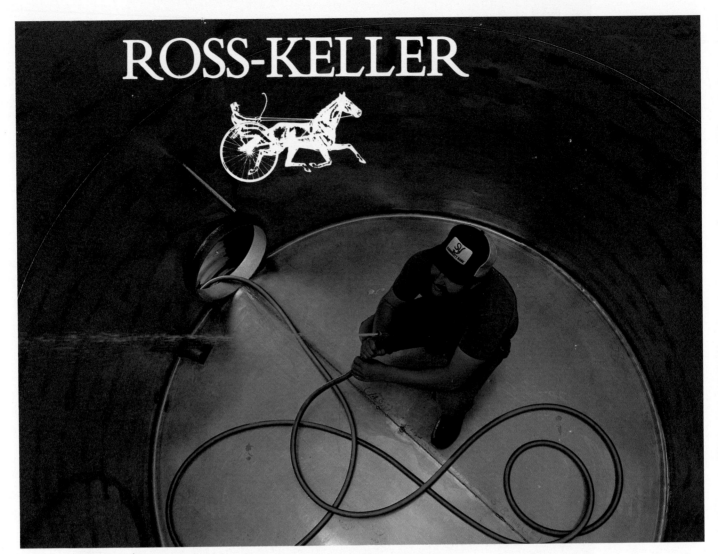

Between the village of Nipomo and the city of Santa Maria is Ross-Keller Winery, an ideal destination for a Sunday outing — or a Monday for that matter. At the end of a eucalyptus-framed lane sit its blue-grey buildings, surrounded by fields bright with lupine in season. Off the tasting room is a sheltered picnic area, adorned with a wishing well.

A tightly-knit family group shares winery duties: oral surgeon Howard Tanner, his wife Jackie, their daughter Tami and their son-in-law Jim Ryan. Jackie, a biochemist, works with Jim to make Ross-Keller's Chardonnay, Chenin Blanc, Johannisberg Riesling, Pinot Noir, Cabernet Sauvignon, Zinfandel and three blush wines — Blanc de Cabernet, Blanc de Pinot Noir and a white Zinfandel.

Ross-Keller gets its name from a German expression meaning "the winery of the horse." "Sixteen years ago, my father-in-law was introduced to Standardbred horses," explains Jim Ryan. "That led to a longtime involvement with raising and racing them. When it came time to name the winery, the association seemed natural." The winery label portrays a racing sulky taken from an 1880s print. Striking as racing silks, the labels were designed by Jackie.

In business since 1980, Ross-Keller Winery buys its grapes from Los Alamos, Shandon and Santa Maria. Small as it is, the winery has gained recognition, especially for its 1981 Pinot Noir. "Winemaking itself is a craft — you get a little better at it every year. Selling wine — that's the biggest challenge," says Ryan. At present, their wines are sold in three counties. ❖

Tepusquet

On a sweeping mesa ten miles southeast of Santa Maria, nearly 1,400 acres of mature grapevines assert their presence. This is Tepusquet Vineyards, the brainchild of veteran grape growers Louis and George Lucas and their partner Al Gagnon. (The partners also grow Tepusquet premium varietals on another 400-acre parcel east of Paso Robles.)

Since the early 1980s, Tepusquet has been quietly building in size and market share. In wine sales alone, Tepusquet's yearly case total is 50,000 and slated to climb to a 100,000-case ideal.

Although the main vineyard appears to be one large piece of identically cultivated real estate, it is not. Vineyard manager Louie Lucas explains: "We've divided it into many smaller parcels, each planted, irrigated, fertilized and harvested individually. That's why we have been able to sell our grapes to so many wineries. And why they have taken so many awards with our grapes." Among the award winners made with Tepusquet grapes are: the 1983 San Martin White Riesling, the 1984 Concannon Chardonnay, the 1984 Callaway Gewürtztraminer and the 1984 Stevenot Muscat Canelli.

Derived from an Aztec word meaning copper, Tepusquet's name is both unusual and striking. Their attention-getting label appears on a full line of wines. In 1983, Tepusquet first entered the wine market with three blends: vin blanc, claret and hock. They have since added a Vineyard Reserve Chardonnay and a Cabernet Sauvignon/Merlot, as well as a line of varietal wines priced for the everyday consumer.

Now sold in 40 states and going international, Tepusquet Vineyard wines are merchandised through grocery stores, wine outlets and restaurants such as the Santa Maria Inn. Their next goal? "A tasting room in the Santa Maria area," say the Lucas brothers. ❖

Santa Ynez
AREA

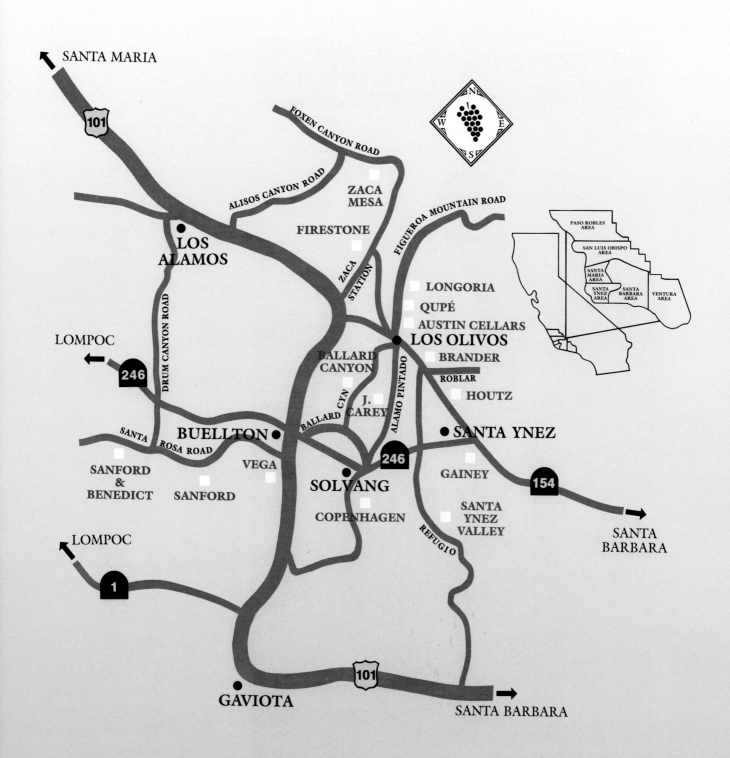

◀ Mission Santa Inés, located in the village of Solvang

Santa Ynez Area

AUSTIN CELLARS

Sweat equity: at his Alisos Canyon vineyard, winemaker Tony Austin does much of the work himself.

"The earth, the sun, the human element — that's the trinity that needs to be great to produce greatness in wine," asserts Tony Austin. Like his wines, Austin is a complex character, passionately outspoken yet fond of understatement. "People look at my label and some of them see that the abstraction at the top is actually an iris — my favorite flower. But look even deeper — and you'll see that the label's background is a topographical map of my 100-acre property," says Tony.

A man of fiery vitality, Tony Austin is considered a formidable winemaker. From a fourth-generation wine growing family in Sonoma county, Tony graduated from U.C. Davis in 1974, in the process becoming the protégé of wine dean André Tchelistcheff. Soon thereafter, he was chosen as the first winemaker for Firestone Vineyard, an association that lasted until 1981 when Austin decided to make his own wines.

Austin Cellars makes Sauvignon Blanc, White Riesling, Chardonnay, Gewürtztraminer and Pinot Noir, and is nearing the 25,000-case-per-year mark.

Austin most definitely does things his way. Rather than put a lot of money into a showplace winery, he has put his resources into his vines and his wines. As a consequence, the winery is a metal building, unpretty and utilitarian. Austin Cellars does have a stylish little tasting room in the village of Los Olivos, off Highway 154.

Tony doesn't believe in the validity of wine competitions, yet he enters them, shrugging: "It's necessary — a new winery needs recognition." Meaningful or not, his walls are covered with awards, including some of the most coveted in the industry.

But Tony Austin is more excited about where his wines end up than how they do in the ribbons ratings. "A wonderful Ojai bed-and-breakfast inn called Roseholm now devotes its entire cellar to Austin Cellars wines," he says gleefully. ❖

> *"My biggest reward? The discovery that people who love wines love my wine."*
>
> — Tony Austin,
> founder and winemaker for Austin Cellars

"**F**un." "Folksy and friendly." "Like a family gathering." These are the kinds of comments routinely received by Gene and Rosalie Hallock, founders of Ballard Canyon Winery. "It's wonderful to get fan letters from people, thanking us. Such appreciation is especially welcome after being a dentist for so many years," says Gene, who retired from his practice in 1982 to devote himself to marketing. "We really enjoy sharing our wines," says Rosalie. "That's why we enjoy putting on events. Like our Harvest Festival, which now runs three weekends in October." The Hallock philosophy of friendly hospitality echoes the history of Ballard Canyon itself,

which in Gold Rush days was located on a stagecoach route.

In 1974, the Hallocks began planting grapevines, at first intending just to sell grapes. By 1978, their plans had evolved to include a winery, which was barely finished in time for their first crush. With the enthusiastic help of their family, nearly 50 acres of grapes have been planted. Ballard Canyon makes Johannisberg Riesling, Fumé Blanc, Zinfandel, Chardonnay, Cabernet Sauvignon, and several blush wines, nearly all from estate-grown grapes. They also make the only Muscat Canelli in Santa Barbara County.

Ballard Canyon has a satellite tasting room in Solvang with a glassed-in patio and tasting bar. From the tasting room, it is an attractive 10-minute drive along Ballard Canyon Road to the winery, where another tasting opportunity awaits. Up a long graceful driveway lined with sycamores sits the winery. An unpretentious structure, it is surrounded with redwood decking and picnic facilities under huge oaks. There is even a row of chairs neatly lined up at the edge of the vineyard, for those who would just like to sit, sip and watch the vines grow. ❖

Yesteryear: now in honorable retirement, this press saw much service at Ballard Canyon and elsewhere. It is capable of crushing three quarters of a ton of grapes at a time.

BRANDER

Grand entrance: a sheltered courtyard and gracious French doors introduce the Brander tasting room.

Single-minded and very French — these words could describe winemaker Fred Brander and his winery, patterned after the estate chateaux of Bordeaux. With its high walls, mansard roof, symmetrical towers and formal tasting room, it looks right. Just one wine is made under the Brander label — a Graves-style Sauvignon Blanc. It is consistency Brander is after. "And that is what consumers want also — a consistent wine, one they can be loyal to, vintage after vintage."

On his 40 acres Brander also grows Semillon grapes, used in his Sauvignon Blanc. "It is the blend which gives the French-style Sauvignon Blanc its character," he stresses. Brander bottled his first Sauvignon Blanc in 1980. Four years later, he received the ultimate compliment.

"Knowing that President Reagan is very supportive of California wines, I brought a case of my newly released 1983 Sauvignon Blanc to his ranch," recalls Fred. "Not only did he call to thank me, the President said he had served my 1982 Sauvignon Blanc at the Summit of Industrialized Nations dinner the prior spring. What's more, none other than François Mitterrand — France's President — had complimented my wine. Now how can I possibly top that?" ❖

J. CAREY

The J. Carey Cellars has that indefinable California country look. To get there, you follow Alamo Pintado Road north from Solvang. At Rancho Santa Ynez, a small sign announces the winery and you turn left, up a driveway fragrant with pepper trees and oleanders. Lush grapevines flow right up to an aged wooden fence. You come to a rusty red winery barn, freckled with holes made by countless woodpeckers. Just beyond is a rambling yellow clapboard house with a tasting room just off its Midwestern front porch and a thick green lawn for picnicking.

In business since 1977, J. Carey Cellars is a 3-generation family enterprise owned by a family of physicians. Four family members are still active in the marketing and management aspects of the winery.

Winemaker at J. Carey is Scott Meyer, formerly with Rancho Sisquoc Winery for three years. Scott's most formative wine experience may be the nine months he spent in Europe, working for a wine négociant. "It gave me a lot of insights as well as a strong desire to come back here," says Scott. "California is really a wine frontier — a place where you are much freer to try new things."

Its vineyards divided into distinct parcels, J. Carey grows most of the Cabernet Sauvignon, Cabernet Franc, Chardonnay, Merlot and Sauvignon Blanc it needs. "We do buy some grapes from other local vineyards to augment our production."

What does the future hold for J. Carey? "We are producing vineyard-designated Cabernet Sauvignon, Merlot and Chardonnay — such as our La Cuesta Vineyard Cabernet and our Adobe Canyon Chardonnay. Our vines — some as old as 13 years now — are really showing what they can do," says Meyer. ❖

With its cosy air of good fellowship, long tasting bar and shop crowded with Old World wines and gift items, Copenhagen Cellars comes across as very Danish. Which is as it should be, since the tasting room is located in the heart of Solvang, a Danish village of windmills and thatched roofs set down in mid-California.

Copenhagen Cellars has been in business on Alisal Street for more than 20 years. During that time, a stream of visitors have found their way to Copenhagen's landmark spire, outlined in firefly lights. From its compact space, Copenhagen Cellars sells a wide

84 Santa Ynez Area

variety of California fruit wines: apricot, olallieberry, plum, pomegranate, strawberry, raspberry and more. It also offers the Vikings IV line of wines imported from Denmark and Germany, such as Danish elderberry and German Ockfender Bockstein. "Because we present unusual wines like mead and May wine (a variety made with an herb called woodruff), visitors can enjoy out-of-the-ordinary tasting experiences here," says tasting room manager Nels Petersen. From herb vinegars to cork pullers, Copenhagen Cellars also has one of the largest wine-oriented gift selections in the area.

Owned by Doug and Candace Scott, Copenhagen Cellars is just part of a larger winemaking and merchandising complex that includes Stearns Wharf Vintners in Santa Barbara and a winery under construction in Santa Barbara County. Because of that relationship, the Copenhagen tasting room also carries the premium varietals of award-winning Stearns Wharf Vintners. In 1985, wines with the Stearns Wharf and Warner West labels took 45 medals. ❖

Santa Ynez Area   85

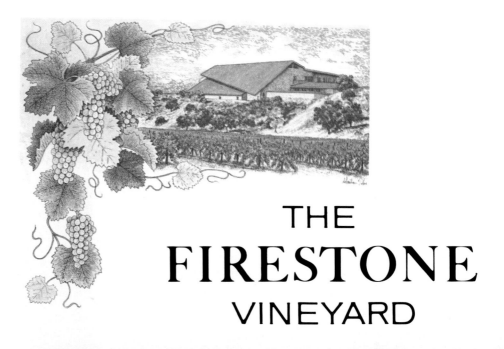

THE
FIRESTONE
VINEYARD

Proud parents: Brooks and Kate Firestone pause against the backdrop of their winery, the result of a decade's hard work.

Granted, other wineries besides Firestone have wealthy owners. Some of them dabble in wine; some direct from afar. A few are like Brooks and Kate Firestone. They have made it their life, tackling both the dirt farmer and the glamour aspects of it with equal zest.

Born into a family whose wealth is synonymous with tires, Brooks spent years as an executive in the family business, finally turning his back on it. "Kate and I wanted to imbed ourselves in a new life, one that related directly to the land," says Brooks. In 1973, he took over a ranch property of his father's and began the slow, painful and expensive process of making a fine winery out of it. He was joined in the effort by his English wife Kate, a former ballerina with London's Royal Ballet, and their four children.

Over the undulating hills of Santa Ynez Valley, 250 acres of grapevines now flow, their green symmetry broken only by the occasional silhouette of a grand old oak. The vineyard raises all the grapes it needs to make 75,000 cases a year of Pinot Noir, Cabernet Sauvignon, Merlot, Riesling, Sauvignon Blanc, Chardonnay and Gewürztraminer. "We may be the leading producer of Johannisberg Riesling in California," says general manager Allen Russell. "However, we are probably proudest of the double gold medal we took at the Club Enologique world competition for our 1978 Chardonnay."

Firestone's first winemaker was Tony Austin, a protégé of preeminent wine expert André Tchelistcheff. In 1981, another Tchelistcheff protégée took on the job: Alison Green. In her teens, Alison had worked as a "cellar rat" at Simi Winery, owned by her father. There she met Tchelistcheff. At his urging, she majored in fermentation science at U.C. Davis, interrupted by stints at a wine research station in France and Hoffman Mountain Winery. In 1977, she began at Firestone, eventually to become one of a handful of women winemakers in the U.S.

On its knoll above the vineyards, the winery looks like a pair of folded brown wings, tips joined to protect a tranquil courtyard. Designed by Richard Keith (architect for Sterling and other Napa wineries), the complex of buildings reveals itself by degrees to tour visitors.

Inside, visitors find redwood walls, sunlight through stained-

glass windows and beautiful details like arched doors with elaborate iron fixtures. Overlooking the vineyard, the tasting room is made bright with Mexican murals and tapestry. But the pièce de résistance is the barrel room. Noble, almost Gothic, its ceiling arches high over 2,800-gallon tanks and what seems to be an infinity of barrels and vats.

Despite being the largest winery in Santa Barbara County, Firestone winery conveys a special aura, the personal stamp of Kate and Brooks. That sense of personality goes deeper than most people realize. "When we began our first construction, I wanted to make a gesture about my feelings to the winery," recalls Brooks. "So I hunted up the silver christening cup that had been mine as a baby. And as we poured the first foundation, I imbedded it in the cornerstone." ❖

Vineyard savvy: from a Northern California winemaking family, winemaker Alison Green has spent years fine-tuning Firestone wines.

Vineyard Visitors

Vineyard thieves come in all sizes. "Next to birds and deer, raccoons and skunks cause us the most loss," says Bill Greenough of Saucelito Canyon Winery. Tony Austin of Austin Cellars agrees: "Raccoons tend to devour the bottom half of each grape cluster, leaving the rest to rot." The vineyards get other medium-sized visitors with the munchies, too. Rabbits and ground squirrels concentrate on the shoots of young vines. Badgers browse on the root systems, undermining the entire plant. But Bryan Watson of Watson Winery believes that gophers are the worst plague. "They can take a 5-year-old vine and chew it in two. We have tried everything — traps, gas, poison, swearing at them — nothing is particularly effective. It's a year-round problem for us." ❖

THE Gainey VINEYARD

Tour attraction: a special vineyard near the winery lets visitors see pruning, trellising and irrigation techniques.

To show the winemaking process from grape to glass: that's the goal of Gainey Vineyards, located near the scenic crossroads of Highways 246 and 154. And Gainey succeeds on two counts. The 12,000-square-foot winery, designed by Robert Lamb Hart and open since 1985, is as logical and beautiful as a nautilus shell. Tours move from the vineyards to the crush, processing and fermentation areas, then on to the vast barrel ageing room and the even vaster 40,000-bottle ageing cellar. At the end of 20 minutes, everyone ends up in the tasting room to sample the finished products.

New but artfully old, the Spanish-style winery is adorned with a wealth of weathered Mexican tiles in all shades of leather. Armoires, tables and other antiques from Southern France fill the tasting area. Intricate chandeliers of antlers add a rugged note; a gourmet kitchen adds an unexpectedly elegant touch.

"We set out to accomplish not just one but a number of things," says Daniel Gainey, owner of the winery and of the 1,800-acre ranch of which it is a part. "First was to design a winery with the visitor's questions in mind. That's why we incorporated what we call the

Visitor's Vineyard. Close to the building, we've planted two rows of each grape varietal. With these vines, we show six different styles of trellising, six methods of pruning and a variety of irrigation techniques. It's the only place like it in California — an education in the vineyard."

"We also wanted to tie in fine wines with fine food, art and music," adds Daniel's wife Robin. "So we included a kitchen to handle gourmet cooking classes, formal dinners and other food-related events."

"Our third goal is long-term: to make the kind of premium wine we know this valley is capable of," says general manager Barry Johnson. "For that reason, we chose Rick Longoria as winemaker. Besides our high regard for his talents, we wanted a winemaker with his degree of commitment to Santa Ynez Valley."

Gainey Vineyards plans to market the lion's share of its Chardonnay, Sauvignon Blanc, Johannisberg Riesling and Cabernet Sauvignon at the winery, via mail order and in a few select restaurants and wine shops. ❖

HOUTZ VINEYARDS

"Peace and Comfort Farm" reads their sign. But it wasn't just peace and comfort that David and Margy Houtz were after. "This place represents opportunity. A way for us to get away from our desks and to express ourselves on the large palette of 28 acres of raw land." That is how former systems analyst Margy and real estate consultant David view their endeavor.

The Houtzes have invested five years of hard work, transforming a former cattle ranch into a green and harmonious

Santa Ynez Area 93

Beyond the barrels: for even the smallest wineries, the exacting process of marketing wine includes label design, printing, trimming and application.

landscape. Sixteen acres of Sauvignon Blanc, Chardonnay and Cabernet Sauvignon grapes trace the gentle slopes of the property. An animal barn, apple trees and a large garden complement the handsome house and redwood winery — all put in by this energetic couple. A focal point is their manmade pond, complete with pergola and resident waterfowl.

"It feels miraculous to create an environment like this," says Margy, whose kinship with birds of every stripe is evident in the tasting-room decor. A multi-talented do-it-herselfer, Margy's sewing skills have created a charming, country-style ambiance for wine sipping. While continuing his Santa Monica business, David has taken U.C. Davis courses and studied winemaking with veteran winemaker Rick Longoria. Their first wines, made with Longoria's help, were released in 1985.

"At Houtz, we're pursuing an estate program, and want to grow to just 3,500 cases a year," says David. "After that, we plan to improve, not expand."

A delightful picnic destination, Houtz Vineyards also sponsors occasional musical and other events. Besides tasting room sales, their wines are sold in restaurants and spirit shops from Santa Ynez south to Los Angeles. ❖

RICHARD LONGORIA WINES

Net profit: nylon netting is an effective way to deflect hungry birds from ripe grapes. The nets snap around the vines and are removed at harvest. Lain Vineyard in Santa Ynez Valley (pictured above) is one of the growers used by Longoria.

One of the winemakers who has left a decided imprint on the Santa Ynez Valley is Rick Longoria. A U.C. Berkeley graduate, he decided on a winemaking career following a visit to venerable Buena Vista Winery in Sonoma. After cellar apprenticeships at Buena Vista, Firestone and Chappellet Wineries, he became J. Carey Cellars' first winemaker. In the past ten years, he has handcrafted fine wines for J. Carey, Houtz Vineyards and most recently for Gainey Vineyards.

In addition, Rick has made small, select lots of Pinot Noir and Chardonnay under his own Longoria label. Although not currently in active production, Longoria vintages will continue to be aged, bottled and sold for some time to come.

"Making wines under my own name has been a long-time dream," says Rick, "one shared by my wife Diana and my father Jules, both of whom are partners in my small enterprise." ❖

QUPÉ

Winemakers can be quirky people — take Bob Lindquist, for instance. Since 1982, he has been leasing facilities — first at Zaca Mesa, then at Los Viñeros — to make several unusual wines under a label no one can pronounce.

"It's *cue* — as in pool cue — *pay*," says Bob, leaning against a case of wine in his meat-locker warehouse. "It's a Chumash Indian word that means California poppy. In 1982, I ran across it in a book of Indian stories and legends. So then I had to find an appropriate illustration. One of my partners is an architect, and sent me a stack of poppy designs. The one I chose is in the Art Nouveau style, done about 1900 by an unknown artist. The poppy was originally stitched on pillowcases."

Bob makes Chardonnay and Syrah (an uncommon red wine, not to be confused with Petite Sirah). He has also made two special blends: a coral-colored wine called Vin Gris, which is 70% Pinot Noir and 30% Chardonnay; and a 3-wine blend called Vin Blanc. He handcrafts about 3,000 cases a year, using mostly European techniques.

Most of his working experience has been in the retailing and tasting-room end of the winery business. "My schooling has primarily been from other winemakers in the area," says Bob.

At present, his wines can be sampled at the Wine Cask in Santa Barbara and at the wine bar in the Santa Maria Inn. A winery is in Lindquist's plans but "with the market as erratic as it has been, I am taking it one year at a time."

It may seem quixotic to pursue winemaking in such a specialized way. But then, Bob Lindquist's alma mater was U.C. Irvine, a school that whimsically calls itself "the home of the anteaters." As he drives away, you notice his license plate: "I brake for anteaters." ❖

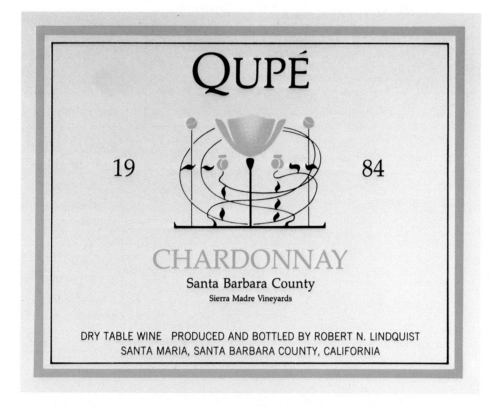

SANFORD

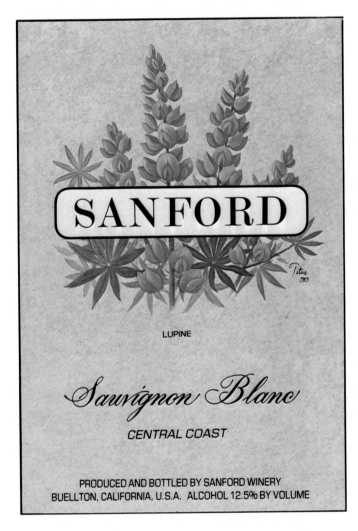

Artistic synergy: the artistry of label designer Sebastian Titus (pictured far right) has meshed with the Sanford wine style to produce a bouquet of beautiful wine labels. Inspired by the native plants around the winery site, the labels represent a botanical library of California wildflowers.

Established in 1981, the Sanford Winery has bloomed as quickly and beautifully as the California wildflowers that grace its labels. Married partners Richard and Thekla Sanford have won as much acclaim for their stylish wines as for their stunning wine packaging, created by Sebastian Titus and Wesley Poole. The Sanfords make Pinot Noir, Chardonnay, Sauvignon Blanc and a copper-colored beauty called Vin Gris from Pinot Noir grapes.

Pleased as they are with their initial reception, the Sanfords are in it for the long haul. On their 738-acre Rancho Jabali, 70 acres of vines are going in, five acres at a time. And up against a valley hillside, a wonderful winery is taking shape. Slowly. "Like the making of good wine, it has taken time to refine our winery plans," says general manager Jim Fiolek. "Richard is a stickler for getting every detail just right."

The largely Mexican workforce is building the 20,000-square-foot winery from adobe bricks made on the premises. "We chose adobe partly for its natural insulating properties — ideal for wine — and partly to produce a structure that seems to grow out of the land itself," explains Richard. The winery also has its own corps of master stonemasons and a carpentry shop where windows and doors are being hand-built.

The Sanfords have a decided tilt toward Mexican and Southwest Indian art and architecture, which is reflected in the winery's appearance and interior decoration. Mexican architect Manuel Parra and Santa Barbara architect Frank Robinson have designed a two-building complex, linked by a large patio with a decorative Mexican fountain and a stage for outdoor cultural events. Besides visiting the tasting room and relaxing in the lounge area, anchored by a huge fireplace, visitors will be able to observe fermentation and other processes

through windows into the production part of the winery. A large cave, carved from the hillside, will accommodate barrels for red wine ageing.

Located five miles west of Buellton, Sanford Winery receives a strong maritime influence, the major reason why the Sanfords chose the area. "But it's not just the Santa Ynez Valley we're promoting — we strongly believe that the entire central coast produces outstanding grapes," says winemaker Bruno D'Alfonso. "So we prefer to blend Edna Valley, Santa Maria and Santa Ynez fruit. To us, the synergy of blending produces a better, more interesting wine."

Richard Sanford, who with neighbor Michael Benedict helped establish the Santa Ynez Valley as a premium grape region, agrees. "The central coast is truly one of the finest viticultural areas in the world. That's because of the unique topography of the region. Our valleys run east-west, allowing the cool winds of the Pacific to flow directly into them." ❖

Local color: the Sanfords — Thekla, Richard and daughter Blakeney — picnic in the flower-studded hills above their winery.

SANFORD & BENEDICT

There is a Zenlike quality about the way that Michael Benedict goes about making wine. Buddhists might call it "right livelihood." "People are sometimes intimidated by the label of 'serious winemaker' that has been attached to me," says Michael. "But my wine isn't just for critics and connoisseurs. What I welcome is sincerity of purpose in a wine enthusiast."

Sanford & Benedict Winery lies near the west end of the Santa Ynez Valley. The access road winds through 113 acres of vines to the venerable winery building — originally a dairy barn. That barn has to be the most soothing man-made structure in all of California. Its only paint is a northside coat of bright yellow lichens. Inside, the barn is cool, dark, fragrant with wine. Most of all, it is musical — musical with the sound of spring water pattering down its tin roof. "This place is very traditional, very low-tech — no electricity, no

Santa Ynez Area

Low-tech and traditionally European: since coming to Santa Ynez Valley in 1971, winemaker Michael Benedict has been making wine in his lichen-covered barn. His goal: to make wines that are worthy of the grapes and soil from which they spring.

stainless steel tanks," says office manager Patti Jordano. The water-cooled roof is fed by gravity flow from a nearby spring. Despite the rainstorm sound effects, most of the water evaporates before it reaches the eaves.

Just off the main room is a splendidly bare tasting room: scuffed wooden floor, a few old desks and chairs and a 100-year-old corking machine as centerpiece. You sit, glass in hand, as the view unrolls itself before you — vines, vines and more vines, only stopped by the brooding La Purísima Hills.

A former U.C. botanist, Benedict searched through the climatalogical data for three states to find this site. He was looking for growing conditions that most closely resembled the Burgundy region of central France. With fellow academic Richard Sanford, he bought this 700-acre parcel in 1971 and began planting. From the outset, Michael has been a serious winemaker, intent on using traditional Burgundian techniques. His vines are dry-farmed, producing low-yield, high-intensity fruit. His wines are big, full, slow to reach their peak. Michael, like other serious winemakers in California, strives to make great Pinot Noir, Chardonnay and Cabernet Sauvignon. He also makes a rosé from Pinot Noir and a dry Riesling he calls "La Purísima." Can serious wines find a serious audience? Fortunately, yes. About 10,000 cases a year are sold by the winery, mostly to restaurants, wine shops and via mail order. ❖

The green, gently swelling acres of Santa Ynez Valley Winery have seen more than their share of state history. During California's Mexican era, the 300-acre property was part of a huge, 36,000-acre land grant. Later, in the early 1800s, the first college in the state was built here. For 80 years, "El Colegio de Nuestra Señora del Refugio" provided education for priests. Still standing from that era is a chapel, now incorporated into a family home. In the 1920s, the Hunt family bought the property and operated it as a dairy for 50 years.

In 1969, a 2-family partnership began to plant vineyards on the land, an experimental move that was extremely successful. "From the outset, we were able to sell our grapes to major wineries such as Paul Masson," says Bill Davidge, a second-generation partner. From grape growing, it was a short and logical step to winemaking. The old dairy buildings made fine winery rooms, and the huge milk tanks became the winery's first fermenting vats.

Bonded in 1976, Santa Ynez Valley Winery gained almost-immediate critical acceptance for its first wines — notably a Sauvignon Blanc and a Blanc de Cabernet, made by Fred Brander.

"We now have 110 acres under vines, growing more than enough for our own needs," says viticulturist Lee Bettencourt. "Our wine line has expanded to include Chardonnay, Gewürztraminer, Johannisberg Riesling and Merlot."

Winemaker since 1984 is Mike Brown, an Australian whose

background includes a degree from U.C. Davis and tenures at California and Australian wineries. "Our emphasis is quite straightforward," says Mike. "We concentrate on premium varietal wines, very drinkable and modestly priced. We also maintain our Reserve de Cave designation for small lots of wine that receive special treatment." One of the nicest places to sip Mike Brown's handiwork is on the winery's outdoor deck, overlooking the vines.

As long-timers in the valley, owners Boyd and Claire Bettencourt and Bill and Dean Davidge have seen a fair amount of wine history in the making. "We own the oldest commercial vineyards in the Santa Ynez Valley. But one of our greatest pleasures has been to see the growth of other vineyards and wineries in this lovely place. We've seen it gain recognition as an outstanding viticultural area. And we are confident that the end is not yet in sight." ❖

Valley skyline: at vineyard's edge, great towers of stainless steel cradle Santa Ynez Valley wines. At the same time, other white and red wines age in oak barrels.

Vega Vineyards

Next to Highway 101 near Buellton sits a Victorian carriage house, largely unnoticed by the traffic hurrying past. This is Vega Vineyards, named for the rancho of which it was a part. Here, owners Bill and Jeri Mosby have created a home and a thriving winery with 31 acres of vineyards. A Lompoc dentist for many years, Bill has been "fooling around with winemaking" since 1959. He and Jeri got serious about it in 1979 and bought the 270-acre property, at that time a horse ranch.

Vega Vineyards makes four wines: Pinot Noir, Chardonnay, Johannisberg Riesling and Gewürztraminer. "My favorite is our dry, Alsatian-style Gewürztraminer," says Bill. "We wanted to fill a niche, and that wine does it. I'm still not completely satisfied with any of our vintages yet. So I continue to experiment." His future plans include making a Pinot Noir Blanc and increasing production to a maximum of 10,000 cases.

About 50% of Vega's output is sold through the tasting room, presided over by Jeri. "We sell the rest through restaurants,

Recycling the past: located in an old carriage house, Vega Vineyards Winery honors its origins, right down to the perky mailbox. Like other growers, the Mosbys (preceding page) fight the birds for the grapes, occasionally doing battle with owl and hawk kites.

distributors and mail order — largely in our 3-county area." The long bar in the small tasting room comes from an old bridge timber. Only half-joking, Jeri says, "We never throw anything away. That's why we had to buy the ranch — we needed a bigger junkpile!" In fine weather, tasters can sit outside and watch the hawks wheel over the hill that seems to protect the winery.

The building interior is neat and compact; upon request, visitors can see the lab, fermentation room and bottling line. When the Mosbys first bought, they attempted to restore the carriage house, long considered an architectural classic.

"We had just begun, and a 100-mile-an-hour wind blew this way," recalls Bill. "Our poor building instantly turned into a pile of lumber — which we've since reassembled."

The jaunty air of the winery, with its rust-red clapboard and whale weathervane, provides a vivid contrast to the family adobe, tucked among cactus, oaks and sycamores. The Mosbys and their three sons and one daughter have spent years restoring the adobe for their use. Built in 1853, the adobe housed the de la Cuesta family. They planted vineyards, a few of which are still bearing today.

"Both the adobe and the carriage house have been landmarks in this valley for years," says Jeri. "Some day, we hope that Vega Vineyards will become the same sort of landmark." ❖

ZACA MESA

One of the area's largest wineries lies almost hidden in the S-curve of an oak-shaded country road. The serene setting corresponds to its name: Zaca is a Chumash Indian word meaning "peace." "And 'mesa' is where we grow our best grapes," says winemaker Ken Brown. "The vines like the soil and climate of our mesa tablelands. There, they get the coolness they

All-rounder: with Zaca Mesa since its inception, winemaker Ken Brown has had a hand in it all, from building design to quality control.

need — and the struggle." He continues: "To make the best wines, you want small berries and clusters. In France, they achieve that goal by planting 3 to 4 times the number of vines per acre than do Californians. So we emulate the French." With 240 acres under cultivation, Zaca Mesa stresses its vines with special pruning techniques and a high number of plants per acre.

In business since 1975, the winery averages about 65,000 cases a year of Chardonnay, Sauvignon Blanc, Johannisberg Riesling, Cabernet Sauvignon, Pinot Noir and Syrah. The 1,500-acre property was purchased in 1973 by Marshall Ream, an ARCO executive who wanted to retire from the oil industry. Ken Brown met Ream while studying enology at Fresno State. Shortly after Ken graduated, they joined forces. Ken designed Zaca Mesa's first winery along with architect Bruce Beckett. The new building, finished in 1981, was a collaboration between architect David Klages and Ken.

Outside, the winery presents a rustic appearance. Of cedar planking, the 22,000-square-foot building forms a U-shape around an informal, flower-bright courtyard. Just inside, a sunny, high-beamed tasting room invites visitors to taste and browse among gift items.

The high-tech production area offers a contrast to the exterior. A maze of huge open-top fermenters, stainless steel tanks, catwalks and 1,800 wooden barrels greet the eye. Among the items Ken is proudest of are the overhead dejuicing tanks for white wine. "Very expensive, but they eliminate bitter phenolics, so we end up with a rich creamy finish on our Chardonnay wine."

In its first decade, Zaca Mesa has zigged and zagged. "In 1981, we embarked on an ambitious marketing program to make three quality levels of varietal wines. We've since opted to make a smaller quantity and only focus on premium and reserve quality. The choicest small lots go into our reserve program," says Ken.

Despite his immense knowledge of winemaking and his evident success at it, Ken Brown comes across as a modest man with a philosophy that debunks a lot of the mystique of winemaking. "More than anything, a winemaker is a glorified babysitter. His job is to keep the wine from getting into trouble. Of course, the wine's personality can be modified. That's what some of the fancy equipment is for. But by the time the grapes hit the crusher, most of what the wine is going to be has been decided." ❖

Santa Barbara
AREA

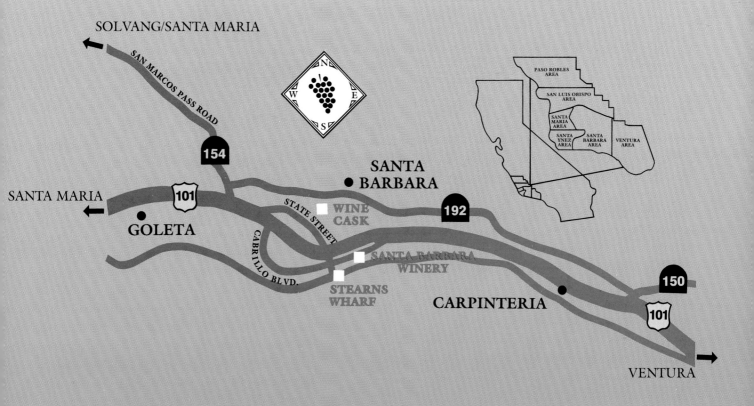

◀ Mission Santa Barbara, located in the city of Santa Barbara

SANTA BARBARA WINERY

Five minutes from the beach, the casual patio of Santa Barbara's oldest winery welcomes visitors. Like the gracious city it is based in, Santa Barbara Winery has a tradition of continuity and a growing sophistication. Founded in 1962 by architect Pierre LaFond, for years the winery produced unpretentious bulk and fruit wines. Two decades later, the winery has its own 70-acre vineyard along the Santa Ynez River and a growing reputation for top-notch varietal wines.

A mark of Santa Barbara Winery's growing interest in quality is its label program. As winemaker Bruce McGuire says, "We wanted local artist Mark Shields to convey the color, flavor and texture of our wines, while giving a regional feeling also. So Mark painted his watercolors with each specific wine in mind. In some cases, he studied the wines from crush through the ageing process." The results have been much applauded. "We now market high-quality art prints of our 1984 Chardonnay label also," says marketing director Julianne Poirier.

But pretty packages do not a good wine make. It has taken years of hard work for Santa Barbara Winery to overcome its "sweet fruit wine" image. "Our wine line now goes in two directions," says Bruce. "We make a number of wines that appeal to the new

wine consumer, such as White Zinfandel, Cabernet Sauvignon Blanc, Johannisberg Riesling, Sauvignon Blanc and Chenin Blanc. And we have a serious reserve program of Cabernet Sauvignon, Zinfandel, Chardonnay and Pinot Noir."

The vineyard, meticulously planted and tended for 14 years by veteran grape grower Bill Collins, now fulfills a major portion of the winery's needs. "However, we do continue to buy some grapes from cool microclimates like our own," adds McGuire.

With the winery since 1981, Bruce McGuire is an experienced winemaker whose background includes tenures at Souverain, Fieldstone and R. and J. Cook Wineries. During his years with Santa Barbara Winery, he has made a number of well-received wines. In 1983 alone, his wines took 15 medals in California competitions.

Santa Barbara Winery is now moving toward production of 25,000 cases a year. Besides tasting room sales, the wines are sold in restaurants and wine outlets statewide. As seems natural, Santa Barbara Winery staff are enthusiastic promoters of the area also. "We are familiar faces at the important functions — from the Vintners Festival to the popular Santa Barbara Museum of Natural History Tasting each August," says Julianne Poirier. ❖

> *"The hardest thing about being a winemaker is the waiting. Waiting all summer long for the harvest. Waiting on wines. Waiting to see what the finished product will be like."*
>
> — Bruce McGuire, winemaker at Santa Barbara Winery

STEARNS WHARF VINTNERS

At first glance, Stearns Wharf Vintners appears to be a simple tasting room on Santa Barbara's popular wharf. Natty and nautical, it offers a congenial tasting bar, light foods and a second-story outdoor deck with a spectacular view of the harbor. At the bar, Stearns Wharf and Warner West wines are available for tasting. In addition, an array of local wineries' products are sold by the bottle.

Stearns Wharf is just one part of a winemaking and merchandising complex that includes two tasting rooms (one in Solvang), two wine labels, a winery in the building stages and a distribution network based in the Midwest. Doug Scott, owner of the operation, has a vision about

California wines. His philosophy? People-responsive marketing. "In 1984, for instance, we made four Chardonnays, each in a different style, each with grapes from different vineyards. Then we collected feedback from all the people who visited our two tasting rooms. With that kind of data, we have been able to fine-tune our wine styles to meet consumers' preferences, not just ours."

This strategy has met with success with the public. "From our central warehouse in Michigan, we are beginning to distribute to other states in the Midwest. In 1986, both the Stearns Wharf and Warner West labels began to be marketed to other parts of the country," says Scott.

How have the two labels fared from the wine-judging perspective? "Very well indeed — for 1984 vintages alone, we received 45 awards from major competitions. In fact, all our 1984 wines received silver medals or better," comments Doug. Stearns Wharf wines include Sauvignon Blanc, Chenin Blanc, Johannisberg Riesling, Gewürztraminer and Cabernet Sauvignon. Warner West offers the same varietals.

Since 1981, Scott has bought grapes and leased winery facilities. Part of that is due to change. "We'll always buy grapes," says Doug. "However, when we eventually open our winery in Santa Barbara County, we'll complete the circle." ❖

"Négociant" or wine broker is the term the French use to describe someone who brings together four things: a winemaker, a label, grapes and a goal. By that definition, the Margerum brothers are négociants. For some years, they have been producing select lots of Chardonnay, Riesling and Pinot Blanc under the striking Wine Cask label.

But they are also the co-owners of two wine retail outlets and a restaurant with its own wine bar and cellar, all called Wine Cask. If that weren't enough, they provide free information on wine events, tastings and tours, produce and sell a Santa Barbara County wine map and promote local wines through exclusive distribution and sales by the glass. Somehow the Margerums also find time to sponsor a series of events called "Dinners with the Winemakers," often showcasing local talent. Small wonder that Santa Barbarans look at the Wine Cask as the nerve center for things oenological.

Younger brother Doug handles most of the management tasks. Hugh Margerum, a Humboldt State fine arts graduate, works principally as an artist. It is his eye-catching abstract acrylics that adorn the Wine Cask labels. What was the original intent of the paintings? "I wanted to create an aesthetic package for the wine, not solely informational. I find many parallels between the making of wine and the making of a painting — both are sensual *and* intellectual experiences. Both are fairly abstract."

Under Santa Barbara County's current licensing laws, tasting rooms without wineries are not permitted. (The two existing exceptions were in business before the law took effect.) Thus the Wine Cask provides a whole range of options not available elsewhere. ❖

"This area has all the elements — climate, talent and soil — to become one of the premium wine-growing regions in the world. We want to be involved in developing that potential in any way we can."

— Hugh and Doug Margerum, négociants and co-owners of the Wine Cask

THE BUBBLY

Long ago, the land east of Paris was open fields — **campus** in the local dialect. Eventually it became a province, but people still called it **champagne.** (The word **champagne** came from **campus** by way of **campania** and **champaign** — people weren't that fussy about spelling in those days.)

In Champagne was a Benedictine abbey, whose wine cellar was run by a monk named Dom Perignon. You may have heard that Perignon "put the bubbles into champagne." What he did was more far-reaching than that. At that time, winemakers had a pretty terrible reputation because no one knew how to seal bottles. What was good wine in September might be vinegar by January. Perignon had a corker of an idea: the cork. With corks, he could store wines from previous years. And he could make sparkling wines, such as champagne.

Which brings us to champagne's main mystery: how **do** they get the bubbles in there? First they make a base wine, then add yeast and sugar and allow it to ferment in the bottle a second time. This produces carbon dioxide gas, which rushes out with tiny drops of wine when you pop the cork.

Party-goers have long sought a glass to keep champagne fizzy. In 1660, the shallow-bowled coupe or tazza was invented. Its rollicking shape is the one we most often associate with New Year's Eve. Later, the tall flute glass became popular. Today's drinkers of the bubbly often favor a long-stemmed goblet in the shape of a half-opened tulip. ❖

Ventura
AREA

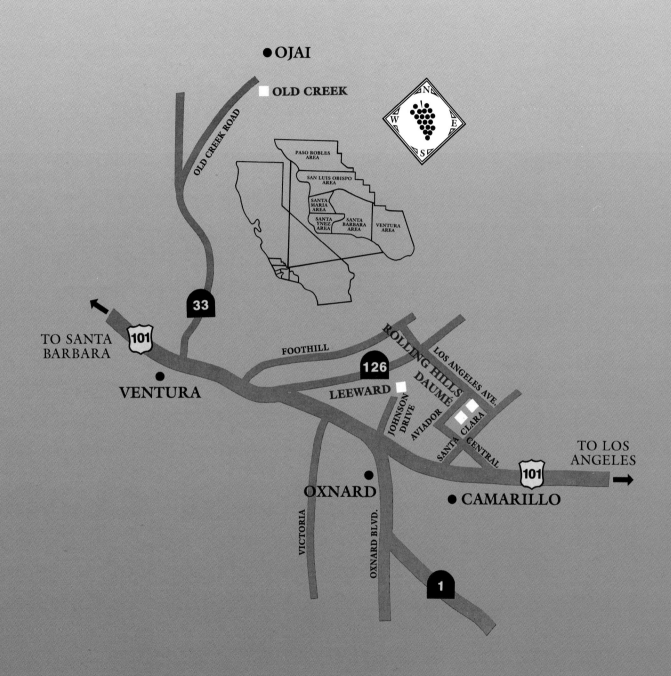

◀ Mission San Buenaventura, located in the city of Ventura

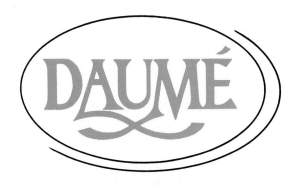

Part of the process: all of Daumé Winery's grapes — including the Pinot Noir — go through a Zambelli stemmer/crusher.

An industrial park may seem an unlikely setting for a winery. But that's where you'll find three out of four Ventura County wineries. Daumé is one of them. Bonded in 1982, the 2,000-case-per-year winery has all the equipment to make premium wine in one compact space, from a French oak barrel room to a bottling line. There's even a barrel-top set aside for wine tasting, which is an appointment-only proposition.

Owner and winemaker John Daumé makes Pinot Noir, Chardonnay, Sauvignon Blanc and a Vin Gris, which he describes as a dry blush wine from Pinot Noir. Since 1970, he's been the owner of a home winemaking supply shop south of Ventura. Making wine was a natural evolution for him. "I see wine as a substance of charm and mystery — quite like an individual," says John. "The challenge is to guide the fruit in the best possible way." Public recognition of Daumé's abilities to guide include three silver medals from the Orange County Fair for Chardonnay and Pinot Noir.

Daumé buys its grapes from Santa Maria, Paso Robles and Edna Valley and will continue to do so. John has no plans for expansion to a more picturesque site. As he says, "All the romance is in the barrels and bottles." ❖

Ventura Area

"Winemaking's greatest challenge? To be consistent. Not that we're making peanut butter — but we do want people to have confidence in what they are buying, year after year."

— Chuck Gardner and Chuck Brigham,
Leeward winemakers

It's a bit tricky finding Leeward Winery. From the name, you might assume that it's located on the water. You'd be wrong.

"We *began* on the water. We were the only house on the marina that had its own winery but no boat," recalls Chuck Gardner, half of the Leeward winemaking team. His partner Chuck Brigham adds: "Our home winemaking eventually took over completely. We were even using our refrigerator for cold fermentation."

After a stint in a smaller building, Leeward Winery is now housed in a spacious, 2-building facility within a multi-use park off Johnson Drive in south Ventura. The emphasis is on sparkling cleanliness and precision equipment rather than ambiance. Nonetheless, the two Chucks have created a cool and agreeable tasting area amid the towers of case goods waiting to be shipped. While tasting, you may be greeted by Cuvée the cockapoo or Sirah the winery cat.

Bonded since 1979, Leeward has gained unusually swift and enthusiastic acceptance. Wine critics from Jerry Mead to Anthony Dias Blue to Earl Hunter have praised their releases. Among the 8,500 cases made each year at Leeward are Cabernet Sauvignon, Sauvignon Blanc, Zinfandel and a Pinot Noir Blanc called "Coral." But perhaps Leeward's strongest offerings are the four separate bottlings of Chardonnay they do each year. The Chardonnay grapes come from vineyards in Monterey

all the way south to Santa Barbara County.

Since all grapes are purchased, the Leeward winemakers are very exacting in shopping for vineyards. "Frankly, I think it is better not to be stuck in one microclimate," says Brigham. They are quick to praise outstanding efforts by growers. "In 1983, the Chardonnay grapes we bought from Macgregor Vineyard in Edna Valley were superior. Not just the grapes but the lengths he and his crew went to get them."

Neither Chuck comes from a winemaking background. Brigham worked in his family's clothing business; Gardner was a Safeway manager. Both men took short courses in winemaking at U.C. Davis.

How has Leeward achieved its results? "The most unusual thing we do is to barrel ferment our wines in a special, 48-degree cold room for up to three months at a time. This prolonged fermentation is like slow cooking instead of 'microwaving' your Chardonnay," says one of the Chucks. "This method is much more laborious, of course." Leeward is one of just two wineries in California to have this type of cold room. ❖

Speed and precision: Leeward has a high-speed foiler and bottling line, an unusual piece of equipment for a winery its size.

Ventura Area

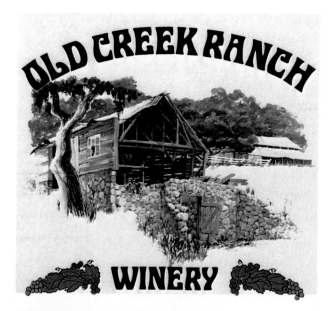

Just nine miles from the junction of Highways 101 and 33 is an idyllic spot, full of enchanted silence. Massive trees, paddocks of horses and flowers give this winery the unmistakable flavor of Ojai Valley. Among its sights are the attractive ruins of the original winery, built in 1898 and being restored. Even if these folks didn't make a drop of wine, this would be a worthwhile destination.

Charles Branham is winemaker and President of a 3-family owners' group. "Besides having the oldest winery in the county, we are proud to be making wine from Ventura County grapes." Using grapes from several counties, the winery makes Gamay Beaujolais, Cabernet Sauvignon, Chenin Blanc, Sauvignon Blanc, Merlot and a prize-winning Johannisberg Riesling.

With its old-fashioned garden of roses, hollyhocks and poppies, the tasting room is an ideal place to sip a glass of Gamay. That is, if you can tear yourself away from the grassy area where visitors are welcome to picnic or barbecue. ❖

Vineyard Visitors

The most unwanted vineyard visitor? Birds. When grapes ripen, they will gobble or ruin 50% of the crop if not stopped. Near harvest, vineyards look and sound like a cross between a carnival and a battlefield. From one row comes the electronically amplified chittering of an Ave-alarm. The next row wears a crazy necklace of balloons and a plastic owl on a pole. Every 15 minutes, another propane cannon fires. Overhead hover ominously-shaped bird kites. "Starlings and finches are so bold and so quick to learn that we have to use many tactics, not just one," says Ken Volk of Santa Lucia Winery. Among other methods, Ken deploys a shotgun patrol and cages baited with birdseed. Other vineyards resort to snap-on nylon nets around vines — costly but effective. Sometimes it takes a thief to catch a thief. A few vineyard owners hire a professional falconer, whose trained hawk can strike terror (at least temporarily) into starling hearts. ❖

Rolling Hills Vineyards

"You don't need a large operation to make good wine." Ed Pagor, owner and winemaker of Rolling Hills, has a point. Working from a 1,200-square-foot space in a Camarillo industrial park, he makes a thousand cases a year of four California varietals: Chardonnay, Cabernet Sauvignon, Merlot and Pinot Noir. "Plus an occasional Zinfandel."

In business since 1981, Pagor has won a clutch of gold, silver and bronze medals at the Orange County Fair and other major winejudging competitions. Of these awards, Ed is proudest of the recognition given his Chardonnay.

Rolling Hills relies on traditional methods: use of the basket press, use of small barrels, and barrel fermentation. And on traditional ways of getting things done; when needed, the whole Pagor family pitches in to help.

The winery uses grapes purchased from Tepusquet and other Santa Maria area vineyards. So why is the winery located so far from the grape source? Ed's answer echoes the feeling of closeness shared by many wineries, large and small, along California's coastal heart. "We wanted to be near the other wineries in Ventura County — especially Leeward and Daumé. We get so much from each other: advice, support, morale-boosting and just plain friendship." ❖

The crush: Rolling Hills gets its grapes from Santa Maria area vineyards, which are then crushed at this compact Camarillo winery.

INDEX & RESOURCE DIRECTORY

This is an alphabetical listing of the wineries and wine-related enterprises covered in the book. Many wineries have special wines or bottle sizes sold only at the tasting room; you'll see them indicated at the end of each entry. For further information, call or write to get on your favorite winery's mailing list. That way, you'll receive word about new releases, open houses and other events.

ADELAIDA CELLARS.................... 12
Mailing address: Adelaida Star Route, Paso Robles CA 93446. Phone: 805/239-0190. No tasting or tours at present.

ARCIERO WINERY 13
Located on the south side of Highway 46, 7 miles east of Paso Robles. Mailing address: PO Box 539, Paso Robles CA 93447. Phone: 805/239-2562. Tasting room open daily 9-5; self-guided tours daily 10-4.

AU BON CLIMAT WINERY 66
Located at 2625 Highway 135 near Los Alamos. Mailing address: PO Box 113, Los Olivos CA 93441. Phone: 805/344-3035 (winery) and 805/963-3141 (office). Tasting and tours by appointment only. Annual open house held the day after the Santa Barbara County Vintners Festival in April.

AUSTIN CELLARS 78
Tasting room address: 2923 Grand Avenue in Los Olivos. Mailing address: PO Box 636, Los Olivos CA 93441. Phone: 805/688-9665. Tasting room open daily 11-5. No winery tours. **Ask about specials and limited releases at tasting room.**

BABCOCK VINEYARDS.................. 67
Located at 5175 Highway 246, Lompoc CA 93436. Phone: 805/736-1455. Tasting room open Fri-Sun, 11-4:30 and by appointment Mon-Thurs – call ahead. Guided tours Fri-Sun, 11-4:30 and by appointment Mon-Thurs. **Ask about the 1985 Sauvignon Blanc Reserve.**

BALLARD CANYON WINERY........... 79
Located at 1825 Ballard Canyon Road, Solvang CA 93463. Additional tasting room at Vintage House, 511 Atterdag Road, Solvang CA 93463. Phone: 805/688-7585. Tasting room open daily 11-4; self-guided tours daily 11-4. **Ask about special vintages.**

THE BRANDER VINEYARD 81
Located at the corner of Roblar Avenue and Highway 154, Los Olivos. Mailing address: PO Box 92, Los Olivos CA 93441. Phone: 805/688-2455. Tasting room open Sat 10-4, on weekdays by appointment only. Self-guided tours Sat 10-4, weekdays by appointment only. **Ask about special limited availability wines.**

CAREY CELLARS: see J. Carey Cellars.

CASTORO CELLARS..................... 15
Located at 1829 El Camino Real, Atascadero. Mailing address: PO Box 1973, Atascadero CA 93423. Phone: 805/466-0287. Tasting by appointment only.

CHAMISAL VINEYARD.................. 50
Located at 7525 Orcutt Road, San Luis Obispo CA 93401. Phone: 805/544-3576. Tasting room open Wed-Sun, 11-5. Self-guided tours Wed-Sun, 11-5; guided tours upon request. **Ask about older vintages.**

CONTI: see Tonio Conti.

COPENHAGEN CELLARS-
VIKINGS IV 83
Located at 448 Alisal, Solvang. Mailing address: PO Box 558, Solvang CA 93463. Phone: 805/688-4218. Tasting room open daily 10-6. No tours. **Ask about wine specialty products.**

CORBETT CANYON VINEYARDS....... 51
Located at 2195 Corbett Canyon Road south of San Luis Obispo. Additional tasting room at 335 Shell Beach Road off Highway 101, Shell Beach CA. Mailing address: PO Box 3159, San Luis Obispo CA 93403. Phone: 805/544-5800. Tasting room at winery open Mon-Sat, 10-4:30, Sun 12-4:30; Shell Beach tasting room open daily 11-4:30. Guided tours 3 times daily Sat-Sun, twice daily rest of the week. **Ask about the 1984 Muscat Canelli and 1985 Gewürztraminer.**

CRESTON MANOR VINEYARDS
& WINERY............................... 16
Located at Highway 58, 17-mile marker, Creston CA 93432. Additional tasting room at the northwest corner of the intersection at Vineyard Drive and Highway 101, Templeton. Phone: 805/238-7398 (winery); 434-1399 (tasting room). Tasting room open daily 10-5 except winter, Wed-Sun, 10-5. Tours by appointment only. **Ask about San Simeon Cellars white Zinfandel and Creston Manor Pinot Noir.**

THE DAUMÉ WINERY.................. 118
Located at 270-D Aviador, Camarillo. Mailing address: PO Box 594, Somis CA 93066. Phone: 805/484-0597. Tasting and tours by appointment only.

EBERLE WINERY........................ 18
Located 3.8 miles east of Highway 101 on Highway 46 east, near Paso Robles. Mailing address: PO Box 2459, Paso Robles CA 93447. Phone: 805/238-9607. Tasting room open daily 10-5; guided and self-guided tours daily 10-5. Tours for large groups should call for appointment. **Ask about the Muscat Canelli.**

EDNA VALLEY VINEYARD 60
Located at 2585 Biddle Ranch Road, San Luis Obispo CA 93401. Phone: 805/544-9594. No tasting room. Guided tours Wed-Sun, 10-4:30.

ESTRELLA RIVER WINERY............. 21
Located along Highway 46 east, near Paso Robles. Mailing address: PO Box 96, Paso Robles CA 93447-0096. Phone: 805/238-6300. Tasting room open daily 10-5; guided tours daily 10 to 4:30. **Ask about older vintages, limited large bottles, special group and catered events and the bargain barrel (good values on less than perfect labels).**

FARVIEW FARM VINEYARD........... 26
Mailing address: Route 2, Box 40, Templeton CA 93465. Phone: 805/434-1247. No tasting or tours.

THE FIRESTONE VINEYARD........... 85
Located on Zaca Station Road, near Los Olivos. Mailing address: PO Box 244, Los Olivos CA 93441. Phone: 805/688-3940. Tasting room open Mon-Sat, 10-3:30. Guided tours Mon-Sat, 10-3:30. Tours and tasting by appointment for groups of 10 or more.

THE GAINEY VINEYARD................ 90
Located at 3950 East Highway 246, Santa Ynez. Mailing address: PO Box 910, Santa Ynez CA 93460. Phone: 805/688-0558. Tasting room open daily 10-5; tastings every 15 minutes. Guided tours daily, every 30 minutes, 10-3:30. **Ask about the Cabernet Sauvignon, Pinot Noir and Merlot.**

HALE CELLARS: see Los Alamos Vineyard.

HMR ESTATE WINERY 28
Located 4.5 miles west on Adelaida Road from Lake Nacimiento Drive, Paso Robles CA 93446. Phone: 805/238-7143. Tasting room at 1245 24th Street, Paso Robles CA 93446. Tasting room open daily 11-5 winter, 10-6 summer. Winery tours by appointment only. **Ask about Franken Riesling and occasional wine library releases.**

HOUTZ VINEYARDS 92
Located at 2670 Ontiveros Road, Los Olivos. Mailing address: PO Box 542, Los Olivos CA 93441. Phone: 805/688-8664. Tasting and tours by appointment only, 12-4 on weekends and holidays.

J. CAREY CELLARS...................... 82
Located at 1711 Alamo Pintado Road, Solvang CA 93463. Phone: 805/688-8554. Tasting room open Tue-Sun, 10-4. Tours Tue-Sun.

LAS TABLAS WINERY 29
Located on Las Tablas Road, 1.8 miles west of Highway 101, Templeton. Mailing address: PO Box 697, Templeton CA 93465. Phone: 805/434-1389. Tasting room open daily 9-5. No tours.

LEEWARD WINERY 119
Located 1/4 mile east off Highway 101; take Johnson Drive exit in Ventura. Mailing address: 2784 Johnson Drive, Ventura CA 93003. Phone: 805/656-5054. Tasting room open weekdays 10-4 and most weekends 10-4; call ahead. Guided tours available same days and hours. **Ask about occasional special vintages.**

LONGORIA WINES: see Richard Longoria Wines.

LOS ALAMOS VINEYARD
& HALE CELLARS....................... 68
Located at 2625 Highway 135, 4.5 miles north of Los Alamos. Mailing address: PO Box 5, Los Alamos CA 93440. Phone: 805/344-2391. Tasting room open Mon-Sat, 10-4:30, Sun 11-4:30.

LOS VIÑEROS WINERY INC............ 70
Located at 618 Hanson Way, Santa Maria. Mailing address: PO Box 3, Santa Maria CA 93456. Phone: 805/928-5917. Tasting room open Mon-Fri, 10-4, and by appointment. Guided tours upon request.

MAPS:
   of California: inside front cover
   of Paso Robles area wineries 11
   of San Luis Obispo area wineries 49
   of Santa Barbara area wineries 109
   of Santa Maria area wineries 65
   of Santa Ynez area wineries 77
   of Ventura area wineries 117

MARTIN BROTHERS WINERY 30
Located at Route 2, Box 622, Buena Vista Drive, Paso Robles. Tasting room at Highway 46 east and Buena Vista Drive, on way to winery. Mailing address: PO Box 2599, Paso Robles CA 93446. Phone: 805/238-2520. Tasting room open daily 11-5 after July 1986. Guided tours: call for hours. **Ask about the annual Mozart Festival special vintages.**

MASTANTUONO WINERY 31
Located at Highway 46 west and Vineyard Drive, Templeton. Mailing address: 1555 Willow Creek Road, Paso Robles CA 93446. Phone: 805/238-1078. Tasting room open daily except major holidays, 10-5 winter, 10:30-6 summer. Please call or write for tour appointment. **Ask about special vintages.**

MISSION VIEW VINEYARDS
AND WINERY 34
Located .8 mile east of the San Miguel Mission, San Miguel. Mailing address: PO Box 129, San Miguel CA 93451. Phone: 805/467-3104. Tasting room open daily 11-5. Self-guided tours daily 11-5.

OLD CREEK RANCH WINERY 121
Located at 10024 Old Creek Road, Oakview. Mailing address: PO Box 173, Oakview CA 93022. Phone: 805/649-4132. Tasting room open Fri-Sun, 10-5, and by appointment other times. Self-guided tours Fri-Sun, 10-5, and by appointment other times. **Ask about the 1984 Johannisberg Riesling and the 1982 and 1983 Merlot.**

EL PASO DE ROBLES WINERY
& VINEYARDS INC 20
Located on Highway 46 west at Bethel Road, Paso Robles. Mailing address: PO Box 548, Paso Robles CA 93446. Tasting room open daily 10-5 winter, 10-6 summer.

PESENTI WINERY 36
Located at 2900 Vineyard Drive, Templeton CA 93465. Phone: 805/434-1030. Tasting room open daily 8-5:30; self-guided tours Mon-Sat, 9-5. **Ask about special vintages and varietals.**

PRESSOIR-DEUTZ WINERY 55
Located at 453 Deutz Road, south of Arroyo Grande. Mailing address: PO Box M, Arroyo Grande CA 93420. Phone: 805/481-1763. Tasting room hours: call summer 1986 for specifics. Tours by appointment.

QUPÉ WINE CELLARS 95
Mailing address: PO Box 440, Los Olivos CA 93441. Phone: 805/688-2477. No tasting or tours.

RANCHO SISQUOC WINERY 72
Located on Foxen Canyon Road, south of Santa Maria. Mailing address: Route 1, Box 147, Santa Maria CA 93454. Phone: 805/937-3616. Tasting room open daily, 10-4. Guided tours upon request. **Ask about special vintages.**

RICHARD LONGORIA WINES 94
Mailing address: PO Box 186, Los Olivos CA 93441. Phone: 805/688-9804. No tasting or tours.

ROLLING HILLS VINEYARDS 124
Located at 167-L Aviador, Camarillo CA 93010. Phone: 805/484-8100. Tasting and tours by appointment only.

ROLLING RIDGE WINERY 38
Located on Magdalina Drive off N. River Road in San Miguel. Mailing address: PO Box 250, San Miguel CA 93451. Phone: 805/467-3130. Tasting and tours by appointment only. **Ask about the 1981 Beckwith Ranch Zinfandel.**

ROSS-KELLER WINERY 74
Located at 985 Orchard Avenue, Nipomo CA 93444. Phone: 805/929-3627. Tasting room open daily 12-5; self-guided tours daily 12-5. **Ask about special vintages, special events and personalized labels.**

SANFORD WINERY 96
Located at 7250 Santa Rosa Road, Buellton CA 93427. Phone: 805/688-3300. Tasting and tours by appointment only, Mon-Fri, 3:30-4:30. Closed weekends. **Ask about older vintages.**

SANFORD & BENEDICT
VINEYARDS 99
Located at 5500 Santa Rosa Road, Lompoc CA 93436. Phone: 805/688-8314. Tasting and tours by appointment, Mon-Sat. **Ask about older vintages.**

SANTA BARBARA WINERY 110
Located at 202 Anacapa Street, Santa Barbara CA 93101. Phone: 805/963-3633. Tasting room open daily 9:30-5. Self-guided tours daily 9:30-5. Guided tours Wed-Sat-Sun at 1, 2 and 3pm.

SANTA LUCIA WINERY INC 39
Located at 85-B Templeton Road, Templeton. Mailing address: PO Box 638, Templeton CA 93465. Phone: 805/434-2541. No tasting or tours until 1987, then by appointment. **Ask about yearly open house.**

SANTA YNEZ VALLEY WINERY 101
Located at 343 N. Refugio Road, Santa Ynez CA 93460. Phone: 805/688-8381. Tasting room open daily 10-4. Guided tours Sat-Sun on the hour; weekdays, upon request. **Ask about Reserve de Cave, late harvest wines and port-style wines.**

SAUCELITO CANYON VINEYARD 62
Located at 1600 Saucelito Creek Road, Arroyo Grande CA 93420. Phone: 805/489-8762. Tours and tasting by appointment only.

STEARNS WHARF VINTNERS 112
Located upstairs at 217-G Stearns Wharf, Santa Barbara CA 93101. Phone: 805/966-6624. Tasting room open daily 10-6, 10-9 on Fri-Sat (year-round) and 10-9 in summer. **Ask about special vintages.**

TEMPLETON CORNER
WINE-TASTING & DELI 40
Located at 590 Main Street, Templeton. Mailing address: PO Box 867, Templeton CA 93465. Phone: 805/434-1763. Tasting room and deli open daily 10-5. **Ask about periodic specials.**

TEPUSQUET VINEYARDS 75
Mailing address: Route 1, Box 142, Santa Maria CA 93454. Phone: 805/937-2043. No tasting or tours.

TOBIAS VINEYARDS 41
Mailing address: PO Box 733, Paso Robles CA 93447. Phone: 805/238-6380. Tasting by appointment only. **Ask about the 1982 Dusi Zinfandel, the 1982 Radike Zinfandel and the 1982 Jones Ranch Petite Sirah.**

TONIO CONTI 42
Mailing address: Adelaida Star Route, Paso Robles CA 93446. Phone: 805/238-5706. No tasting or tours.

TWIN HILLS RANCH WINERY 44
Located at 2025 Lake Nacimiento Drive, Paso Robles CA 93446. Phone: 805/238-9148. Tasting room open daily except holidays.

VEGA VINEYARDS WINERY 103
Located at Highway 101 and Santa Rosa Road, Buellton. Mailing address: PO Box 62, Buellton CA 93427. Phone: 805/688-2415. Tasting room open daily 10-4; guided tours daily 10-4. **Ask about special selection of Gewürztraminer and Johannisberg Riesling.**

WATSON VINEYARDS 45
Located on Adelaida Road near Paso Robles. Mailing address: Adelaida Road, Star Route, Paso Robles CA 93446. Phone: 805/238-6091. No tasting or tours. Send name and address to get on mailing list.

WINE CASK 114
Two locations at 813 Anacapa Street, Santa Barbara CA 93101, phone 805/966-9463; and at 1290-A Coast Village Road, Montecito CA, phone 805/969-3955. Hours for Santa Barbara wine retail store: Tue-Sat, 10-10; Sun 12-5; Mon 10-6. Restaurant and wine bar: lunch Tue-Sat, 11:30-2:30; dinner 5:30-10 Fri-Sat, 5:30-9 other nights. Closed Sun-Mon. Montecito store: open daily 12-8.

YORK MOUNTAIN WINERY 46
Located on York Mountain Road off Highway 46, 7 miles west of Highway 101, near Templeton. Mailing address: Route 2, Box 191, Templeton CA 93465. Phone: 805/238-3925. Tasting room open daily except major holidays 10-5. Tours by appointment only. **Ask about gold and silver medal winners.**

ZACA MESA WINERY 105
Located on Foxen Canyon Road near Los Olivos. Mailing address: PO Box 547, Los Olivos CA 93441. Phone: 805/688-3310. Tasting room open daily 10-4. Guided tours daily at 10:30, 11:30, 12:30, 1:30, 2:30 and 3:30. **Ask about magnums, 375ml and other releases.**

By its very nature, a book cannot keep pace with real-life events. While accurate when we went to press, you will find as time goes on that some wineries in the book will have changed hands or direction. The number of central coast wineries is also growing faster than we can document. To add to your wine-tasting pleasure, we suggest calling the following wineries and vintners which do not appear elsewhere in the book.

BELLI & SAURET VINEYARD, Estrella Star Route 4360, San Miguel. Phone: 805/467-3885.
BYRON VINEYARDS, 5230 Tepusquet Canyon Road, Santa Maria. Phone: 805/937-7288.
CARRARI WINES, P.O. Box 556, Los Alamos. Phone: 805/344-4000.
CLAIBORNE & CHURCHILL VINTNERS, 2585 Biddle Ranch Road, San Luis Obispo. Phone: 805/544-9594.

Ihe wineries of San Luis Obispo,
Santa Barbara
and Ventura Counties.

California's best-kept secret.

Until now.